MIDNIGHT STREAMS

To Be A Saint

by
Michael J.
Hoogasian

I continue to give thanks and praise to the Lord Jesus Christ for his sacrifice and grace that have allowed me to persevere through a difficult time of loss and transformation. Coincidentally, I dedicate these thoughts and ideas to all my family, whose immense love and support will not be forgotten.

Printed by Lulu.com 2011

ISBN: 978-0-557-31107-1

A Sharkangel Book

SHARKANGEL

The SHARKANGEL symbol combines the author's reverent connection to St. Michael the Archangel, guardian of Christ's faithful, and his childlike fascination with great white sharks.

Special Acknowledgement:

I thank God for my incredibly generous, blessed, and gifted Grandma. She gave me her own written revelations to use as I deem fit. The insight within her manuscript is priceless. I have prayed that the messages within have been faithfully revealed to those to whom He wills. Some of the themes, ideas, and poems of Midnight Streams: To Be a Saint were inspired by her moving words and certain lines have been incorporated into these pages.

"Yet the Lord will command his loving kindness in the daytime, and in the night his song shall be with me, and my prayer unto the God of my life." (Psalms 42:8 KJV[1])

Regarding Midnight Streams

No doubt, we have all been up late at night, past a normal bedtime hour when deep thoughts and ideas are running rampant. During these restless times, our speech tends to flow freely in both familiar and strange company. We become vulnerable to sharing secrets, perceptions, and experiences that under different, more natural circumstances would be locked away in our mind's vault. Honesty seems so easy, while trust and confidence a guarantee. Alone, it is within these moments, during these so called "ungodly" hours, where many life-altering decisions and events may occur. Inspiration stimulates its greatest visions, provoking the genius within to have such amazing feelings of insight and creativity.

"Midnight Streams" is a phrase I use to capture the essence of the cognitive events that transpire during such occasions. Thoughts, though often sporadic, flow in *streams* of consciousness concerning all aspects of life. Frequently influenced by a particular day's occurrences, ideas regarding daily and life-long choices, social interactions, senses of duty and purpose, the search for meaning in an otherwise meaningless existence all generate an uneasy mind not settled yet for sleep. Amidst such confusion, organization is necessary to quiet many unanswerable questions and give peace to a weary head. Moreover, it is at these times, I feel, prayer is most useful and effective when applied with contemplation and patience. Writing becomes a highly beneficial tool in these situations, providing sense to sometimes overwhelming conceptions.

"The Lord is my shepherd; I shall not want. In verdant pastures he gives me repose; beside restful waters he leads me; he refreshes my soul. He guides me in right paths for his name's sake." (Psalm 23:1-3 NAB[2])

I wrote the preceding preface for my first book <u>Midnight Streams – Spirited Discovery of Flowing Insight</u>[3] back in 2003 to describe the overall nature of its ideas. It was an extension of the poem that bears the title of these books I have been called to write.

My own 'midnight streams' flowed rather smoothly for a handful of years after writing that manuscript. My restless thoughts and prayers were abundantly answered with direction in the acquisition of my newly found career as a coach, teacher, and devoted man. I was on a good path, a 'right' path…

"Beloved, do not be surprised that a trial by fire is occurring among you, as if something strange were happening to you." (1 Peter 4:12 NAB)

…However, complacency left me on a plateau where I patiently, yet foolishly, awaited an expected transition. Startling circumstances brought about by complicated choices turned my world upside down. I was suddenly confronted with an enormous test of faith instead of the joy I had anticipated. It seemed I was being called to something different from my expectations and personal plans. At the beginning of my great sadness, by some mysterious intuition I found myself suddenly face to face with the following troublesome, yet comforting, declarative message: "care not that you have been rejected. *I* caused it. *I* have other plans for you." An inner peace told me to trust the puzzling sentiments and to keep praying. And so, through the aftermath of the most difficult time in my life, streams surged through tormenting memories, broken promises, destroyed dreams, baffling contradictions, and betrayed emotions from within and without.

Among them all, Vengeance, Wrath, Despair, Doubt, Disappointment, and Solitude dared to seize my mind and my very soul. Though in spite of their brutal attacks, the quiet reassurance of God's presence whispered in my heart at the darkest times: "I am closer than close, nearer than near..." Being human caused occasional grief and emotional setbacks, but by His eternal grace, the following streams share revelations from deep within that will illustrate the necessity of perseverance along our righteous paths. Coupled with that, the love of God and for God is paramount and becomes life's ultimate motivation. Truly, faith allows us to accept it when He tells us, "…My grace is sufficient for you…" (2 Corinthians 12:9). So, as you struggle with your tests, whatever they may be, I write now that you may learn what you need to learn by His grace from these words. May God bless you in all your good endeavors for the Glory of His Holy Name; and in the Holy Name of Jesus, I pray for you, my reader. Amen.

Midnight Streams

Underneath a bright moonbeam

Minds swept away by a midnight stream.

Such calm waters under the sun

Storm after the day is done.

Flowing by all that you want,

Regretful choices torment and taunt.

Foggy memories along the shore

Enshroud lost loves you once adored.

Tossed and turned from side to side

Unleashed in your mind, no place to hide.

As rapids rage, then begin to dive

Within the mists continue to strive

And beneath cascades of midnight streams

Find, at last, your lifelong dreams.

To Be a Saint…

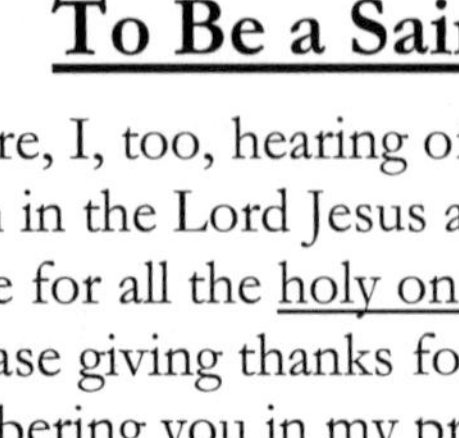

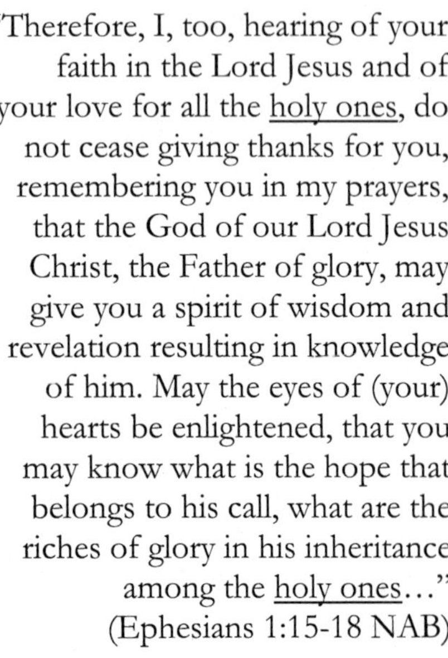

"Therefore, I, too, hearing of your faith in the Lord Jesus and of your love for all the holy ones, do not cease giving thanks for you, remembering you in my prayers, that the God of our Lord Jesus Christ, the Father of glory, may give you a spirit of wisdom and revelation resulting in knowledge of him. May the eyes of (your) hearts be enlightened, that you may know what is the hope that belongs to his call, what are the riches of glory in his inheritance among the holy ones…"
(Ephesians 1:15-18 NAB)

My first book, Midnight Streams – Spirited Discovery of Flowing Insight, discussed many ideas that pertained to walking a path in life that is uniquely designed for someone to follow according to his/her *God*-given talents. Poems and personal discourses elaborated on concepts such as uncertainty, faith, free will, consequences, and the appreciation of various blessings. Similarly, this book contains several poems that illuminate various qualities of saints and circumstances that may face them. Likewise, I have inserted some personal thoughts on the nature and significance of other relevant ideas. Bible verses that spoke to me in times of distress and meditation instructed me on virtues like perseverance, focus, forgiveness, and selfless behavior.

So, along those lines of thought, I have long been fascinated by the meanings of words. I often find myself searching dictionaries and thesauruses for explanations and alternative expressions of words that intrigue me. One such word that has been heavy on my mind during this tremendous season of my life is "saint." In common usage, it simply refers to any individual who acts kindly toward others. If you are nice, pleasant in speech, and generous, (especially in times of overwhelming odds) then you are so labeled.

Surely, everyone has encountered men and women of all walks of life who fit this description. They make life more enjoyable for others and offer hope to the discouraged. It's just their apparent disposition. Evidently, their destination is heaven, and naturally, I hope to see them there and be counted among them.

In religious circles, the term takes on a more significant connotation. Having been raised as a Roman Catholic, my understanding is that the Church recognizes a Communion of Saints and canonizes exceptionally blessed individuals as revered Saints. The former doctrine describes the incredible relationship among the faithful on Earth, souls in purgatory, and those in heaven. These saints share the bond of salvation that comes from faith in Christ, sealed by their common baptism and ultimate destiny to receive eternal life in heaven. They are able to share in a divine communication network to benefit the entire body of Christ through prayer.

The latter requires more scrutiny into the life of a noticeably more spiritually gifted person. These individuals are typically recognized posthumously by experienced church leaders after evidence from their lives is investigated and conclusively found to be extraordinarily blessed with the grace of God. Upon sufficient proof, the Church honors their lives of extraordinary service and devotion to Christ and His teachings. These unusually pious people are then sanctified, i.e. recognized as holy, and given special places among the faithful. Prayers may be said to them to assist with petitions to God the Father through Jesus, seemingly not unlike how someone might ask you to pray for others that need some sort of help. While these brief descriptions may leave you with questions about the complete explanations of the Catholic Church's teachings, it is not the intention of this work to elaborate on them. For more detailed (and probably more precise) information about these and other Catholic doctrines, I suggest reading through the Catholic Encyclopedia[4], Catechism of the Catholic Church[5], various Catholic apologetics, historical writings of the church founders, and/or ask a local priest for more information.

In most Christian organizations outside the Catholic Church, the word "saint" simply refers to anyone who professes Jesus as Lord and Savior. These "holy ones" are mentioned throughout scripture and seem to be synonymous with disciples of Jesus. Like all religious matters, the definition of "a saint" is another disputed one between different sects of Christianity and other religions, who have their own traditions regarding "saints" as well. In an attempt to avoid disagreements over technicalities or other rivalries, (thank you, Titus 3:9), let it be clear that throughout *this* book for my own reasons, "a saint" refers to one who behaves unselfishly in terms of intent and action because of a deeply rooted faith in God. As you read on though, you'll definitely see my clear deliberate connection of the term to faith in Jesus as the Son of God, too.

† † †

Once the reality and certitude of my unwanted and unexpected transition sank in, I was left with a void to fill. Having been a God-fearing man for as long as I can remember, I needed answers on how to deal righteously with my grievous and potentially unrighteous choices as well as discerning when and if I had made some. From every examined human perspective, my actions were gracious and justified when faced with my apparently all-too-common dilemmas. And yet, from every angle I was simultaneously guilty of grievous sin in light of Jesus' words on the matter. Despair and Solitude concentrated my mind's thoughts on the axiom "damned if you do and damned if you don't." Life made no sense anymore.

In constant prayer I searched the scriptures for solace despite its conviction and was given the grace to understand that by faith a saint: "is saved if you do and saved if you don't." This phrase surely has raised some eyebrows for those Christians reading this that disagree with salvation by faith alone. Again, I am not writing this book to argue or defend a position per se, but mainly to share a testimony to the mercy and grace of God. There are many details and qualifications that accompany situations people face to discern the correct course of action given all available information. The failsafe of all saints is faith. By faith saints strive to fulfill the will of God the Father like Jesus so perfectly did. Due to our propensity toward error, we *will* make wrong choices, but God will make good of it regardless and be ever ready to forgive when we realize by His Holy Spirit that we've erred. It is the understanding of our offense toward God that drives us to approach the Throne of Grace boldly (Hebrews 4:16) seeking mercy, in which we are made righteous by Jesus' intercession. Moreover, if we happen to choose wisely and do well the first time, we are saved having been blessed with the capacity to make the right choice; that should be logical. Either way, a saint's action made in faith will result in the glory of God.

As this wisdom of God penetrated my heart and embraced my troubled mind, which seemed to constantly work against me, my focus began to drift from my personal problems to deeper theological concepts. I eagerly read more and more of the New Testament, both the New American Bible and the King James Version, battling with my own Catholic faith and the ideas of other sects. Deciphering differences and wrestling with interpretations of many doctrines between various flavors of Christianity kept me busy for some time. Take my word when I say that it is enough to drive a person insane and is probably why most people avoid those topics with such good cause.

Well, while I flirted with that disaster often, the notion of salvation was of utmost concern given the nature of my dilemma to which I previously alluded. This inevitably led to several passages that shouted to me the qualities of being a saint, i.e. a person to whom salvation was granted. But, as I have mentioned, faith plays an incredible role; one that frees the soul to rejoice in the truth and have moments of such clarity that everything negative seems to essentially disappear. So, although I may have been close to the brink, because of the mercy and grace of God, I was never truly falling over the edge into madness and each facet of the trial has been and is tolerable.

So, I continued to diligently seek the kingdom of God as Jesus tells his disciples to do. Meanwhile, I became more and more intrigued by passages discussing saints or "holy ones" depending on the translation I was reading. While the Gospels tell frequently about how to become one of God's people, Paul writes so eloquently on how to become better ones and to help others become them, too. The faithful followers must live a certain way, remove vices, be prepared to respond righteously to situations, to give thanks for everything (perceived good and perceived bad), and be able to show and encourage others to do the same. They essentially learn by the Spirit to sacrifice themselves completely to do the will of God as Jesus demonstrates in His selfless life, ministry, and ultimately in his death. This education of a saint appears to be an ongoing process, probably not perfected this side of heaven. However, the process does seem to allow saints to live selflessly to a degree that is literally supernatural for regular people or those who merely put their faith in themselves.

† † †

In all my studies and experience, given a premise of free will, there is only one cause for the type of noble behavior saints display. That is love. I have become utterly convinced that no such thing can exist in mankind without a loving God. Human society and basic instinct dictate selfishness, self-preservation, self-promotion, etc. And given the choice alone, free from external influence, I think everyone would choose in favor of his or her immediate self-comfort rather than in favor of someone else's. I haven't found a satisfactory evolutionary, psychological, philosophical, or other human explanation for altruism, and yet it is demonstrated throughout the world by the efforts of *God-fearing* people. There are so many people around who just give and give and give without any discernible reward for their efforts. These can only satisfactorily be explained by love rooted in a faith in a God that loves His creation and has its best interests at heart. Also, I see a direct connection between the characteristic of God-fearing and genuine compassion: to have a *fear* of God is to be in awe of Him. This begets a reverence which produces faith. Faith bestows gifts and blessings from God, the greatest of which is love (1 Corinthians 13:13).

Since this love ultimately comes from God, the reflection and expression of it in its natural state is for God. Since God requires nothing for His own satisfaction of existence having a perfect love for Himself, love's greatest expression is in loving other people because they are the ones that need it. I think this is why

God would command it to be spread so voluntarily and freely (Matthew 22:36-40), even for enemies (Matthew 5:44).

This brings to mind an interesting encounter I had with what I believe to be God shouting at me. After a few months of the reality of my loss settling in, I became depressed, lost, and unsure of what to do with my life. My faith had grown (although frequently attacked by doubt) at least to a point where I seemed at peace with what happened and was assured of God's enduring love for me. With a greater appreciation for Christ's sacrifice and redemptive work on the cross, I often found myself praying "Lord, I love you, but I don't know what to do; it hurts so much; please just come and take me home." Coincidentally, and I use that term facetiously, I found myself a few hundred miles from "home" visiting family in the Vermont mountains. By "chance" I sat in a very small church in the middle of nowhere at just another Sunday mass, having wrestled the 5 hour drive and day before with restless thoughts like the ones stated above. And yes, *coincidentally,* I stood with a slight tear forming in my eye and a smirk beginning to tease itself across my weary face when the Gospel story and homily was from John 21. For those of you unfamiliar with the passage, after Jesus is raised from the dead, he spends some time with his apostles. He asks Peter three times if he loves Him, to which Peter says in no uncertain terms, "of course!" For the previous few weeks I had been wallowing in self-pity and self-condemnation, but the priest that day emphasized and preached (seemingly directly) to me that here Jesus wasn't asking Peter if he remembered the three times he denied Him a few days back. Jesus was smiling in my mind's eye as He asks Peter if he loved Him. Each time Jesus asks, when Peter replies, Jesus tells him to tend his sheep. Be skeptical if you so choose, but in those moments I realized that God the Almighty Creator of Heaven and Earth was just giving me a signal that He had been listening. "If you love me, Michael, then do your job: look after the sheep in your care as best you can (middle school/high school teacher) in spite of these temporary circumstances. I hear you, and I am with you. Remember, I am greater than it all, closer than close, nearer than near." My faith continued to grow.

The continuous examinations of scripture and the inner sanctum of my soul, concurrently with instances of spiritual awareness like the one described above have resulted in my ever increasing faith in Jesus the Son of God. I have perceived a great intensification of my faith in terms of knowledge, understanding, expression, and passion as a consequence for seeking answers in His Word and through prayer in response to my own trials. Having been doing so, I believe God has granted me a certain level of appreciation of the nature and dynamic distribution of His Spirit dwelling within the hearts of believers (1 Corinthians 12; John 3:8). It is God's gift to those who place their faith in Him. It instills a sense of compassion and selfless duty, allowing an individual to do things according to the merciful and self-sacrificing will of the Father as opposed to the selfish personal will of fallen man.

After prayerfully reading the New Testament a handful of times in a rather short span, I also began recognizing saints walking among us everywhere. Some are more easily identified than others, while I believe some don't even know that they are saints…yet. God's Holy Spirit is working in and around each of us at all the millions of different places we happen to be along our life journey. Therefore, until it is ALL said and done, no one, save God, is ever in a position to judge the soul of a person (1 Corinthians 4:5). We see them partially in time, changing with time, yet He judges from an eternal perspective, unchanging and whole.

And therein rest both a liberating bit of truth and a troubling fact to ponder. When someone sins against us, we can be quick to forgive and forget. We know by faith that in time God's Spirit will move the person back into a state of grace or ultimately carry out His divine justice with an omniscient analysis of the person's heart. However, the sins of others cause great pain and sorrow for seemingly blameless individuals. Sometimes forgiveness is granted without apologetic or repentant prompting, but the damage of the sin lingers causing further suffering. How much suffering is patient endurance sharing the sufferings of Christ awaiting the repentance of a transgressor versus needless self-punishment that steals the joy of Christ from a living saint? Certitude on this issue is certainly a matter of perspective, and the resolution is most definitely a matter of faith. However, whenever I allow my mind to dance in circles on the issue of anger toward the unfairness of life's circumstances, or whether or not to hold grudges, streams eventually and again *coincidentally* exhaust themselves by falling on truths found in Matthew 6:12, 14-15; Mark 11:25; Ephesians 4:31-32; and Luke 23:34. If you don't you're your Bible nearby, essentially, the path toward inner peace, that is, the true peace within yourself and with God is forgiveness. You have all heard the saying, "nobody is perfect." Well, that includes you too. So, whatever he or she did, no matter how selfish, heinous, vile, or wicked… let it go. If you don't already, you're going to want someone to grant you forgiveness sooner or later. Let it be contagious because life is too precious, too dear. Let love rule your heart and show you the Way.

† † †

Returning now to the idea of this supernatural gift of love, I have also noticed that saints frequently face obstacles that impede the works of this gift. At times, circumstances seem so impossible to overcome, that all progress of good works stop, and despair seems like the natural state of mind. "What's the point?" "Why do I even bother?" "Life sucks, then you die," "the rich get richer and the poor get poorer," "one man or woman can't really make that much of a difference," and other negative frames of mind blur the senses, even among saints. It causes even the best of them to lose faith. It turns out… that even saints, ones blessed and chosen by God Himself, are indeed merely men and women.

Often times, though, without even a logical answer, something happens that carries them through the worst trials imaginable. This can only be explained by God's mysterious grace, which significantly separates a sinning saint from a saintly sinner. It would appear that some good people do evil and some evil people can appear to do good. Faith allows one to see how all of God's "mysterious ways" work together for the good, especially when the result takes you through trials designed to not just test, but to strengthen that faith. Faith also allows a person to hope and encourages him/her to keep going because it is known deep down that things are going to get better, that things really do happen for a reason (not just any reason, but a meaningful and beneficial one).

This mentality is crucial because there are forces at work against saints in many forms of constant worldly opposition. Selflessness is so often crushed by someone else's selfishness. Kindness is so easily taken advantage of, exploited, or left unappreciated. Surrounded by so many stories of wickedness flourishing and obtaining wealth, it is easy to think that the struggle one puts himself/herself through just isn't worth it. No greater cause than love can appear to merit the type of self sacrifice people make because of genuine love. These types of temptations seem to mock compassionate individuals endlessly. Soldiers, dedicated teachers, social workers, one or another partner in a relationship, small businesses, etc… so many people are walked all over and often blamed for problems completely beyond their position's descriptions. It's not fair… at least, not on the surface. However, faith dictates that God has the final say, and everything simply is just not done yet. In the end, the faithful are assured that all will be brought to light and all will be made right. Out of love, these selfless individuals push forward against such difficult opposition, but it takes a great amount of faith.

In a time of great sadness and loss, I considered my own situation in a humble profession that receives little respect and whose fruit is often never perceived by the person who helped cultivate it. It would have been so easy for me to throw in the towel, to start looking after myself, and become a bitter faceless individual in a crowd seeking personal glory. I certainly had the means, but I had fortunately been grounded at a young age in the concept of God's love. The little faith that was left in my heart when it was completely shattered was still enough to know better, and the midnight streams started surging again. Finding occasional solace through the sympathies of friends and relatives, I found far more potent reassurance in God's Word. And so, after having read through some of my introductory thoughts about saints, I invite you to engage the waters that followed months of prayer and reading. Ponder the thoughts within these streams. Though every word has been measured carefully, they seem to me to have been poured forth from a deep seated wisdom that surprises me more often than when I sit and think about what I feel like writing. While I consider much of my prose to sometimes be just a rambling conglomeration of just one more guy's opinions passing intermittently through my brain (ya, like that), I feel the poetry is something more poignant. Either way, enjoy…

† † †

"Here is the patience of the saints: here are they that keep the commandments of God, and the faith of Jesus." (Revelation 14:12 KJV)

To Be a Saint

It baffles the mind why almost all mankind
intensely yearns
for all the things at every turn
that destroy him quickly, it's sickly,
how they rarely learn.
Pay attention to this here lesson,
for in His wisdom there is redemption.
Call to mind the saints…

They have no reason or intent to lie,
faith beyond reason, and heaven bent to try
to open the eyes of the blinded host
of all peoples coast to coast
in need of the grace of the Holy Ghost.

Think about them everyday,
heed the model they display,
See their actions play by play:
wiping tears of the broken hearted,
consoling kin of the departed,
courageous skills among evils,
empty lives they intend to fill,
while shouting sermons from the tops of hills.
Meek but not weak,
as narrow paths they seek.
A bit beyond flesh, approaching spirit,
what you suffer, they can bear it,
writing a hymn of angels, you should hear it,
just let sin go and do not fear it.
Love is the way, Peace is the end.
Simple it seems, but I'll say it once and say it again:
Think it's easy? To be a saint? It ain't...

Being humble,
it's tough not to stumble,
there are things to fall on,
under the pressure; it's easy to crumble
in overwhelming times of sorrow and remorse,
resisting such opposing force,

while sin and death
try to smother every breath.
The worst you could do is to remain still,
where you are, indifferent there to all the poor, the ill,
those who kill and steal to get their fill.
Take a minute…
ponder the infinite,
get some perspective of why you're here.
Contemplate and be reflective
then realize you must choose to give
your time for others' care.

And with that in mind, now take a look
at the Good Book,
see how to live like the saints do live:
Saul's future lay on a different path,
a higher path, away from wrath.
It became obvious now, so clear somehow, amazing, wow!
By the Law he thought he had the light
but still had blinded sight,
he was never right,
but then ready for flight,
he would end your plight,
and was on guard to fight
the evil plagues that surround you,
attacking all around you.
Let the grace he received, find all you too.

That's just a sample,
their deeds are ample,
a setting example
like that guiding star in skies afar,
showing the way,
giving hope each day.
Always on their best behavior,
they're joyful, waiting for the Savior.
With self control, just know their role:
to steal back souls from devils' coals.
Letting sinners burn not
for the sins they've wrought,
forgiveness is all the hope they've got.
Tickets to heaven they should've bought,
not sold their souls for all they sought.
But believe it or not,
it isn't worth the fate you meet,
down that dead end street,
you will be beat,
knocked off your feet
before you know it,
and too many have already died
with absolutely nothing to show for it.
But think it's easy? To be a saint? It ain't...

Listen while I illustrate the fate
of the state of mind
it takes to be constantly kind
and make one great…

Temptation is all around,
its limits are now unbound.
Demons to the left of you, Demons to the right of you,
you're so unsure of what's left of the fight in you.
Constant vigilance demanded,
defy compliance or be reprimanded,
there's no acceptance,
you must accept this: have no excess.
It's tough to explain but I'll expand it:
just be candid.
Though you'll be forgotten and not paid,
left alone and rotting in your trade.
Memories of your good deeds fade,
The world is expected of you,
but expect nothing
except to be rejected.
You have to hold on, be strong,
love carries on,
and it bears it all,
so stand up tall
after every fall.
Go day to day living on nothing but faith.
Endurance tested, patience tried,
duties endless, until you've died
you'll be restless, almost friendless,
persecuted for piousness
and oppressed for righteousness.
Misunderstood, with intentions good,
cock-eyed stared at like you're not aware that

it's so unfair, what you'll see

just letting be some sins to be,

it ain't easy, trust in me.

because in sinners' eyes

it is wrong to read the Word, love the Lord,
follow along, sing Him a song...

SATIS! ENOUGH!
It is time to show those sadists who is really tough.

You cannot dream of what it means,

the amount of will to remain still

on the straight and narrow,

feel with your marrow

the compassion needed to forgive **all**

after the way you have been treated,

the saints, Christ's who won't ever be defeated.

See the Bible, read it.

It's all in there. So do you care?

If you only knew the sacrifice in spite of strife,

the love above and grace bestowed,

the patience granted and nothing owed

but the recognition, a sense of blessing,

the fact that you have learned a lesson.

We're here to share the love, the care, now if you dare,

come follow Him, even on a whim,

it might seem grim,

but get swept away,

come seek The Way,

confess your hate, remove the taint,

profess your faith, *and just be a saint*.

The Support of & Counsel for a Saint…

"Now faith is the substance of things hoped for, the evidence of things not seen. For by it the elders obtained a good report. Through faith we understand that the worlds were framed by the word of God, so that things which are seen were not made of things which do appear." (Hebrews 11:1-3 KJV)

I can't say enough about faith. The more I think I understand it, something else happens that gives it another dimension. Soon after the completion of my undergraduate studies, I wrote much of my first book. As I contemplated my purpose and delved deeper into my pursuit of God, I attempted to define faith according to my understanding and experience. By my own words, "Faith is a pure unbound motivation allowing a person to endure and continue through any tribulation."[3] I look back on that statement post-personal-tribulation and think, "Hey, that's not bad… fairly insightful for a 22 year old without a clue." I have an even greater appreciation for it now having had my faith severely tested. That kind of faith has carried me through some intense emotional anguish and spiritual distress. It was also during this time that I read, studied, and learned more about the benefits of this faith that is continuously tried, strengthened and deepened.

Through a series of intimate encounters with faith, many universal truths were illuminated. Faith for saints is strongly concentrated on the goodness and love of God and His will for their lives. However, in this confusing sport we call life; people can have faith in many different things besides God. Typically, they will have a certain level of trust in other people, themselves, and ideas or things that have seemed to provide consistently for them. This simple trust is associated with faith, but unfortunately tends to lead to disappointments of all sorts.

I used to think it was logical to assume that it is unlikely for anyone to place his or her faith in something he or she knows little about. As I view modern society, I surmise that many people place little faith in God and don't place much emphasis on His role in their lives. I thought perhaps so many people have a general lack of faith in God because they rarely take the time to learn about Him through prayerful search. Sadly (from my perspective) I see so much more faith being placed in scientists, doctors, and drugs (medicines) to set a person's life straight. Strangely though, I imagine that the general public has little knowledge or understanding about how their procedures, mechanisms, and chemicals produce their desired effects. There's even less knowledge about the side effects, which, in the case of medicines, are typically negative. Despite this, there is an almost innate trust placed in the guidance and recommendations from those experts and their methods. What are the side effects of faith in God? Hope? Joy? Patience? Peace? Why isn't there a basic understanding of trust like this in everyone's heart for God? I certainly don't know; does anybody know? Maybe there is, but we're just not conscious of it…? Maybe we are all blind until He chooses to reveal Himself to us? Maybe it must be learned? Whatever the case, I feel it necessary to at least ask such questions.

Something else I've observed: if and when an individual finds out some negative aspect about their object or subject of faith, it is natural for that person to lose some faith in it. This loss of faith, a shaking of confidence, or shred of doubt is inevitable when it comes to faith placed in people and things of the world. As wonderful as someone or something may appear, he, she, or it is fallible and likely to let someone down eventually. As these situations shape our perceptions, our own unsteady wills alter our level of faith in those things. Consequently, this life is filled with trust being shifted constantly from one thing to another as situations change. This makes faith a mere delusion, a popular word thrown around to make a person feel better about hopeless and baffling experiences.

I certainly had misplaced some faith in certain individuals, including myself, and unreliable, unrealistic ideals that led to major disappointment. The distress of its recognition put my mind and heart to the brink of abandonment of everything that I had held dear and sacred in this life. I saw nothing that this life could offer, and I just wanted out. Though, suicidal isn't an accurate description for the type of release a person of my faith background experiences. The negativity and corruption of the world and our society causes a deep yearning for God's promised paradise. When life loses its meaning and purpose temporarily, all anyone wants is the madness to end. In the case of saints, it is not necessarily that life is despised, but rather there is an intense desire for the perfection of heaven where God will wipe away every tear and make all things new (Revelation 21:4-5). Bad circumstances cause soreness. According to our faith, nothing of experience in this life pales in comparison to His promise and so like Paul, we become stuck between the joys of fruitful service in this life and the pleasures of the next, which are far better. Nevertheless, by the grace of God, as I cried out to Him, my misplaced faith was shifted from hollow promises and wishful thinking back to the beacon of salvation, namely Jesus. True faith, as I have begun to comprehend isn't riddled with doubt, but rather blessed with mystery and confidently peaceful.

So, after much personal reflection, I have come to the conclusion that there is only one faith that makes any real difference, and it has little to do with the self and its perceptions. After all, what faith is worth anything save faith in a perfect being? Everything is by necessity going to fail us in time. Therefore, if we are going to place our faith in anything or anyone why not put it into the God who made us? If there is any choice in the matter whatsoever and any real virtue called faith, let us pray He hears our prayers and guides us to a blessed life. If He is real and listening, surely a solid faith will result as He does begin to answer our pleas, not with everything we've ever desired, but rather with everything He knows we need. Every other avenue is a lost cause, ultimately ending in partial or complete failure. The degree to which we can learn from our trials or be scarred by them would apparently depend on the severity of the circumstances. *Faithfully* speaking though, no condition is enough to completely overwhelm the senses so long as there is a shred of faith in God.

This faith that saves is essentially put into the idea that God does indeed love us, and if He loves us, it must be true what has been testified about His sacrifice in Jesus and enduring faithfulness despite our faithlessness. But what if He doesn't love us? Well then, what faith or hope does anyone have? In this life full of uncertainty, is it better to have a life full of hope or full of despair? I choose hope. I choose faith in God… and for so many other reasons as my testimony continues beyond the most obvious: "because I need Him."

† † †

As far back as I can remember (still as far back as age 3) God was always a part of my life. Thankfully, my parents taught me and my siblings about morals and brought us to CCD and church as kids. When my Granny died when I was about five, I was very curious about death and recall thinking deeply about it, heaven, and scarily enough even hell. Without knowing much about God or the complexity of belief systems that awaited me as I aged, it would appear that God started me early on my quest for Him. The seed that was planted all those years ago has certainly taken root, and though I would *love* to brag about what a big tree I've become, His spirit just as certainly tells me how foolish it would be to claim such a thing. I am thankful He has given me the desire and energy to pursue Him each day, to learn and grow stronger in His love. Proud that I've come as far as I have passed the pitfalls of youth relatively unscathed and most grateful for having passed through some fire a bit more polished, I am still humbled, given knowledge that I still have a long way to go.

This wonderful faith journey with Him though would not have started had He not been introduced to me by someone who loves me. (Here is just one more reason why we, who are aware of His grace, mercy, and love, ought to share it with many without holding it back). The mere wonder of God is plenty to begin a line of questioning that turns into a life-long search for a deeper relationship with the Almighty. Also, with God at the source of every individual's journey, no matter what place one starts, I believe this kind of genuine questioning/search leads each person eventually to Jesus and the conundrum of His cross. At its foot every individual is challenged with the question that Jesus Himself poses to His disciples in Mark 8:29, "…who do you say that I am?..." The honest response to this question is the most significant turning point in a person's life. For those who accept Him as Redeemer, Savior, Shepherd, Sacrifice, and Lord receive an invitation to step through a newly opened door to a life full of hope generated from a faith that will be fortified by His Holy Spirit.

The phrase "leap of faith" now comes to mind as I have begun to discuss this imagery of going through unknown doors. Growing up, many of us are told to "look before we leap." Various doors are unlocked and opened for us many times throughout our lives, and we take risks, some more calculated than others. And though it might be wise to *always* look before we leap, sometimes it is impossible to know what to expect as a result of some of our choices. No amount of forethought is totally sufficient to predict long term consequences, especially those involving other willful individuals.

However, we only need to be able to look to the extent that we can see who has opened the door and who is telling us to jump. When Jesus is your way, your truth, and your life, your faith dictates that He is holding all the keys, unlocks all the doors, and is ever-present to guide you through every door you choose to walk through. What a comforting gift: to leap into the unknown, knowing His grace is sufficient; His love is faithful and enduring. He is powerful, a mighty and awesome God. ("My Father, who has given them to me, is greater than all, and no one can take them out of the Father's hand." John 10:29 NAB)

† † †

I recall vividly making a conscious decision, i.e. leap, at one point in my young relationship that I was so sure about because of my faith in what *seemed* to be so right. With these glasses that I've been wearing since the second grade, it would seem that hindsight is much clearer than foresight. Regardless, I distinctly remember praying, "Lord, I'm totally convinced You brought her back into my life for this reason. I'm about to make the biggest decision of my life. Thank you for this, and I know if anything goes wrong, You'll be there to carry me through it." The final part of that prayer was barely a whisper in my thoughts, not expecting anything to happen as shocking to me as what did. Truly, God hears every part loudly and clearly. For, after something going unexpectedly and terribly wrongly, I can honestly say, He hasn't left for a second. He knows the burden I carry, "the cross I pick up daily," (Luke 9:23) and He bears most of its weight. Blessed be God forever.

† † †

Scripture is filled with passages about faith and its effects. I spent three months rather obsessively reading just the New Testament, focused on verses that mentioned faith in its relation to salvation. That resulted in a twenty-eight page word-processing document of verses, just verse pasted after verse with minor commentary notes on their content. Certainly, faith is an incredible part of this game of life, and it appears that we have a choice in what or in whom we place our faith. For saints though, the choice is clear: faith must be in God, for as I mentioned before, faith in anything or anyone else leads to inevitable disappointment and ultimate failure.

I have also observed that faith itself is alive. While it is often compared to a rock and a foundation set upon stone, I find myself picturing it as a skeletal structure. In biological terms, circumstances that cause manageable stress intensify the strength of the bones and benefit the calcification process. This makes the bones harder, stronger, and more resistant to breaking. This is a relatively common concept taught in most high school biology classes. It's interesting how clichés like, "whatever doesn't kill you makes you stronger," really do ring true in more ways than one.

This pattern of strengthening from temporary moments of slight injury happens in both the physical and spiritual realms of life. When a person clings to his/her faith when it is tried but not broken, it grows stronger. For instance, we are often faced with circumstances that challenge our faith. These situations add stress and are typically unexpected, unwanted, or both. And since God makes us a promise in 1 Corinthians 10:13, we can be certain that we will not be given any circumstances or temptations beyond our ability to deal with them. He provides a way out so that we may be able to endure. These stresses will thereby strengthen our faith in Him, the gifts He has given, and the integrity of the righteous path on which He leads us. This can only happen when we have faith in Him and the Word that brings us this message.

Another interesting insight from scriptures is the idea that the greatest things in life are gifts. Life is a gift; salvation is a gift; hope, love, and joy are all gifts. True faith is a gift as well. If a person is to endure and overcome ANY period of suffering, the faith that person has, must be placed in God so that it can be received even more abundantly from its natural (or I should say its supernatural) source. It must be tried and strengthened by experience while matured through the study of scripture and through active prayer. The more we get to know who it is we are saying that we trust, the stronger our faith will become in Him because He is fundamentally incapable of letting us down. When we use this gift through good practices, prayer, and reading, He reveals His character and power more readily. Faith grows continuously and He makes Himself known to us most readily in the person of Jesus of Nazareth.

Additionally, events occur from time to time that impact us beyond daily temptations and worldly annoyances. Significantly greater "trials by fire" as mentioned in 1 Peter 4:12 are ones that seem to devastate and crush one's spirit. I am inclined to believe that every saint is *required* to endure at least one major trial like this. Perhaps the more of these saints go through the better their reward after all is said and done. Through these extremely difficult times though, our all-loving God uses such brutal attacks of the enemy to burn away any lingering human doubt in Him, to strengthen us as we cling to Him, and to fortify us into a follower more prepared to meet the challenges of the world. For just as we can count on God to always be faithful to His Word, we can count that His enemy is just as unyielding when it comes to his wicked efforts to thwart God's plans for His saints. That is why saints are told to ask for their *daily* bread and reminded that "we do not live by bread alone, but by every word that comes from the mouth of God," (Matthew

4:4). As God's people, saints need to remain in Him to be nourished, to be kept healthy, and to be in constant connection to Him, mindfully and thankfully. The moment we let go of His guiding hand to get a closer look of what else is out there, a servant of the enemy waits to tempt. And though everyone is tempted, not everyone needs to stray. Instead, saints must rely on their faith to keep them rooted in God's love and promises.

† † †

In the months after the destruction of my joy and heart, I reread my own words in Midnight Streams – Spirited Discovery of Flowing Insight on faith. I became utterly perplexed at how certain individuals close to me could choose what they chose in light of my writings, our experiences together, and things that were said. My own words began to drive me mad the more I focused on everybody else's "foolish" choices. My search for answers yielded constant frustration and cyclical torment as I attempted to ease my rational sense to understand WHY?? this unfathomable heartbreak was happening. Readings from the book of Wisdom, Proverbs, and the many letters of Paul presented guidance that would leave me thinking: "if only those *other* people were reading this, I wouldn't be in such misery over the current situation, and all this pain could be avoided."

Again, I must give thanks to God for my supportive immediate family who were (and are) available at a moment's notice for comfort. They are undoubtedly a generous blessing. I became accustomed to calling my sister 6,000 miles away in moments of intense frustration and pain whenever my mind couldn't handle its own rationalizing and mental gymnastics. So, as I explained these troubling thoughts about the wisdom I was reading to her over the phone one night, she reminded me again that God had a reason for *me* reading those passages at those times, and it wasn't to torture me about what might have been. While I whined in my own thoughts about how this person and that person should be made known of this fact of life, choices, and their consequences to come to their senses, and this whole ordeal just wasn't fair… I began to realize the messages *were* for ME. I was reading them because God knew at that time that I needed to hear those words to understand that He was teaching me to be understanding, compassionate, forgiving, peaceful, faithful, calm, and resilient. *Those* words were meant *for me* to see at that time, just as *my words* are here *for you* now…

When I focused on the thought that God hears our cries for help and answers kindly, my faith reassured me that I was being shown the right way to deal with my troubles for myself. He provided guidance; He showed me that His grace is sufficient when I read through His Word. For the light and hope in my life to shine brightly again, He was showing me how to move on from this unexpected tragedy, this apparent injustice and preparing me to help others in their own misfortunes turn back toward the light of His truth.

† † †

To let go and move forward through any crisis, our minds must be made right. Letting go and truly forgiving people for their transgressions against us requires much faith. Faith in God's almighty power of love to guide us gives us the mindset to view all circumstances as coming from His divine providence. Actually living with this attitude/spirit and not just merely saying we believe it, is what needs to happen. "His grace is sufficient…" For what? To do what it is right despite circumstance. Spiritual grace is most commonly defined as divine help. It is a freely bestowed gift, given at will and portioned out by the Holy Spirit of God. We must choose to accept gifts and use them for His will, not our disobedient selfish ones. My heart's desired responses to sins against me were of intense anger, thoughts of retribution and what I would call "outbursts of *restrained* fury." Thank God for better sense and the grace to respond to these instincts in accordance with the Spirit and not the flesh (see Galatians 5). Prayers of sincerity were met with peace of mind and an ability to sacrifice those basic human reactions. Grace was being poured forth for forgiveness to work its miracles of changing hearts and lives. Thankfully, it has been my heart that has been undergoing the most positive changes in spite of my ignorance of what God might be doing in other people's hearts.

I am grateful for the grace He gave me to see and understand my situation from a more compassionate perspective too because it had a beneficial effect on those around me as well. While I certainly experienced the most pain directly, my family was also severely hurt by the situation. Love makes strong empathetic bonds between family members, and when one part suffers, they all suffer. They definitely felt similar sadness, disappointment, anger, and frustration. Fortunately, my apparent gracious response was to turn toward prayer and the Bible rather than the bottle or something worse. As I prayed and was given peace, it reflected in my behavior and attitude that I shared with my family, especially my mom, as we all dealt with the sudden drastic change in life. I saw myself becoming a stronger person, and my behavior was setting an affirmative example for those around me on how to deal with tough situations. These statements may appear boastful, but I can only assure you that I am humbly grateful that God was (and continues) using me in this manner.

† † †

So, after faith has been challenged and then strengthened, where does one go from there? How can someone avoid looking back and prevent being hurt by the past? How can we live on this faith without falling back into old ways that may have at least partially caused current tragedy?

In my first book I comment on the nature of schemas and the roles they play in shaping our experiences. After having expectations and dreams dashed to pieces, it's difficult to make sense of where to go after accepting the truth of present circumstance. When things do not make sense to the limited amount of knowledge we have, it is good to remember that we do indeed have a very limited grasp on things. It's a definite problem to reconcile all things to one another for the sake of personal understanding of situations that eventually bring a person to the conclusion: "maybe I'm just not supposed to understand now, or even at all."

Even with faith, this is a difficult sentiment to accept. It typically requires a great change of perspective, a submission of will, and even a complete change in schema. To change one's view of the world takes serious will power to abandon will and tremendous faith to let go. For this type of drastic transformation to occur, a metaphorical death of the old schema must happen. Out of death comes rebirth in spirit. The old self must be crucified, must die, must be shed and cast away. There can be no strings attached. If there are, there is always a means to fall back. Rather, by faith we are encouraged to stay focused on the final prize which lies ahead of us (Philippians 3:13).

Since we are still in the flesh until we physically die, there will always be some remnant of the old schema left to taunt and tempt us with negative or unproductive thoughts. Sometimes legal or social obligations may remain, but almost always there will be memories. Being reborn in the spirit in this life, as in my experience, cannot be complete because we are still susceptible to the world's temptations. This is a debated theological concept, one to which of course there is no "answer," just a conclusion again based on faith. Regardless, by faith in Christ and remaining focused on His sacrifice, we are better able to resist these temptations if they do exist and fall penitent at the foot of His cross when we might give in on occasion.

In the recent aftermath of my initial dilemma, I frequently let myself slip down paths of thought that only caused anger and frustration. As I reread my old words on faith and schemas, I automatically applied them to my woes. Before constructive things could happen, I needed to understand that other people and their support are necessary for healthy transitions through difficult times like the ones I was facing. As one significant relationship was ending, I saw several others that surrounded it diminishing too. However, simultaneously I was able to still see God's hand strengthening other relationships, especially in those who witnessed my relatively gentle response to the misfortune. In testimony to this set of circumstances I "coincidentally" attended a Bible study whose topic was Romans 8:28-31. It was certainly comforting again to realize that God was and is actively working in my life. And it truly is an interesting question posed in that final verse: "What then shall we say to this? If God is for us, who can be against us" (Romans 8:31 NAB)?

Again, I must emphasize the idea that God *loves* us, present tense. He is listening, not was or will listen; He does listen; He is listening. While even that idea may be uncertain for individuals at times, I had written in my first book that faith must be developed to thrive amid uncertainty. The uncertainty of life surrounds us and causes fear and doubt. Therefore, faith must be firm and persistent no matter what the circumstance. Since faith is attacked constantly by deceitful contradictions from the world and even our own perceptions, we must consciously and persistently choose to view life through the lens of faith. The unrelenting questions and sources of doubt are tests to distract us from becoming more solid in a most fundamental truth: God IS. If we truly believe that HE IS, just as His proper name "I AM" implies, there is nothing logical, or worse, irrational that should hinder us, and the words of Paul in Romans 8:31 come surging into mind. Faith must be solidified through constant reminders in scripture reading, charitable service, and ceaseless prayer. It is not enough to make a decision to follow the Way and then stop because in our fickle hearts there is always the dangerous possibility to choose the wrong way again. Therefore we must be mindful to constantly choose to seek God in every situation. In doing so, we can rest assured that His grace is sufficient, and He is guiding us every step of the way.

Indeed, whenever my mind began to drift down thoughts of wrath or despair, my prayers were often coupled with petitions for me and others and the responses were of peace. I found myself faced with a choice of dwelling on feelings of rejection, betrayal, and pain or empathy, compassion, and acceptance. Even despite the absolute personal nature of the situation, I was granted the blessing of using the circumstances as merely a grand learning experience for my inevitable future prosperity. During the first realizations of an unavoidable break, I was presented with the only viable option of running and letting run. By His grace I understand that He allowed me to run, not away from my problems, but rather right into His arms. Over the year and a half to two years after the initial tragedy, God has moved me toward a state of forgiveness: for not only for the ones who hurt me by their words, actions and non-actions, but also especially for my own shortcomings. As I continue to pray and follow that path of peace, I am reminded to give thanks to Him always and continue to let go of the lingering intermittent anger that resurfaces. Only with a faith fixed on Him and His love am I able to know that in time the negative effects of the past will cease to have any effect on me at all. Finally, when I was being tormented with restless nights pondering how to respond wisely to my unique, yet all too common problem, the following poems came out of a dusty shoebox of forgotten notebooks and still new streams flowed with holy counsel as well. Each verse, I feel, carries a tune of peace with a sublime purpose. Learn and enjoy…

"Beloved, do not be surprised that a trial by fire is occurring among you, as if something strange were happening to you. But rejoice to the extent that you share in the sufferings of Christ, so that when his glory is revealed you may also rejoice exultantly."(1 Peter 4:12-13 NAB)

Faith

Do you have faith?
In the Word or the feeling?
In the Reality or the dream?
A breath moves with revelation,
You feel Spirit come over you,
Breaking free from within,
It passes through, leaving a blessed scar.
In that moment anything seems possible.
Everything is possible.
You are in stride to conquer the world,
But the feeling fades and you retreat.
What happened to your newborn faith?
Was it in the Word or the feeling?
The feeling is fleeting,
But the Word holds true.
Have no expectations:
Do not fear or look to sense.
Trust, and simply *know*
The Spirit is always present,
Prepared to move at will.

"When you look for me, you will find me. Yes, when you seek me with all your heart," (Jeremiah 29:13 NAB)

"Then he said to all, 'If anyone wishes to come after me, he must deny himself and take up his cross daily and follow me."
(Luke 9:23 NAB)

"for you know that the testing of your faith produces perseverance. And let perseverance be perfect, so that you may be perfect and complete, lacking in nothing."

(James 1:3-4 NAB)

"And not only so, but we glory in tribulations also: knowing that tribulation worketh patience; And patience, experience; and experience, hope:" (Romans 5:3-4 KJV)

Once is Enough

Once is enough,

But not to satisfy.

Just once removes a keystone,

And the first domino has fallen.

Floodgates are cast wide open.

Unstoppable patterns unfold…

Slowly, but surely,

The waters will rise.

You cannot swim forever.

Sink and drown on your own,

Or ask Him for help.

Listen. Once is enough…

But not to satisfy…

Once is Not Enough

Once is enough…

But not to satisfy…

Having heard His call,

You dared to listen closely.

Making an ardent choice,

You initiate the daunting journey,

Wholeheartedly at the onset,

But your faith and strength wane.

Struggling to continue,

surrender seems viable.

No. Once is not enough,

Genuine resolutions are not single acts,

Persistence is incessant choice,

Devotion requires unyielding progress.

The choice must be enduring

Because once is not enough…

† † †

"Jesus said to him, 'have you come to believe because you have seen me? Blessed are those who have not seen and have believed." (John 20:29 NAB)

"Abraham saith unto him, 'They have Moses and the prophets; let them hear them.' And he said, 'Nay, father Abraham: but if one went unto them from the dead, they will repent.' And he said unto him, 'If they hear not Moses and the prophets, neither will they be persuaded, though one rose from the dead." (Luke 16: 29-31 KJV)

"Although you have not seen him you love him; even though you do not see him now yet believe in him, you rejoice with an indescribable and glorious joy," (1 Peter 1:8 NAB)

'Blind' Faith

No, I've never seen a vision, nor heard an angel's voice.
Never felt the precious wounds or been forced to make the choice.
Specters, ghosts, and spirits never came in blazing light,
Nor have shadows, imps, or demons come to spend the night.
Was never carried heavenward from what I can tell,
Nor dragged below to spend a moment trapped in hell.
All the world is filled with doubt,
And most don't know what life's about…
I've crashed and burned, even cursed the days
Sinned and fallen and gone wrong ways,
But as a saint, I will trust the Lord
To guard me so and guide me toward
That peaceful state within this life,
Through every trial and all the strife,
No matter the chance or event to endure
Faith in His Word is always the cure.
All we must do is open up and receive…
For blessed are those who have not seen yet believe.

† † †

"In every thing give thanks: for this is the will of God in Christ Jesus concerning you." (1 Thessalonians 5:18 KJV)

Rejoice in the Lord always. I shall say it again: Rejoice!" (Philippians 4:4 NAB)

"Boast not of tomorrow, for you know not what any day may bring forth." (Proverbs 27:1 NAB)

Living Faith

Let's have no goals, no expectations,

Living faith for the duration.

Wherever we go, the fate we meet,

Are we in His hands or under His feet?

What He grants, we must accept,

May in His thoughts our souls be kept.

When trusting God, no need to fear

It is *all* good, so no worries here.

Grateful, mindful, we must always pray,

Living faith just day by day.

"On this account I am suffering these things; but I am not ashamed, for I know him in whom I have believed and am confident that he is able to guard what has been entrusted to me until that day." (2 Timothy 1:12 NAB)

"Do not let your hearts be troubled. You have faith in God; have faith also in me." (John 14:1 NAB)

"I put no trust in princes, in mere mortals powerless to save. When they breathe their last, they return to the earth; that day all their planning comes to nothing. Happy those whose help is Jacob's God, whose hope is in the LORD, their God," (Psalms 146:3-5 NAB)

"then all of you and all the people of Israel should know that it was in the name of Jesus Christ the Nazarean whom you crucified, whom God raised from the dead; in his name this man stands before you healed. He is 'the stone rejected by you, the builders, which has become the cornerstone.' There is no salvation through anyone else, nor is there any other name under heaven given to the human race by which we are to be saved." (Acts 4:10-12 NAB)

A Leap of Faith to Walk in Faith

Take two of these, and you'll be fine.
No caution needed, just toe the line.
Your heart is strong, your soul divine,
Trust your way, and I'll trust mine.

Buddha's breath, a Shaman's verse,
Mosaic Law, a Voodoo curse,
Vishnu's kindness, a jihad's wrath,
And atheists all rouse Satan's laugh.

There's only one true leap to take
For in its flight there's much at stake.
Jump into Christ, then be secured,
Confident, convinced, assured,
There is nothing any more to fear
With God Himself always near.
Once you've dared to take that leap,
You'll walk in the promise that He keeps.
So breathe in deeply if you must,
Recite your prayer with simple trust,
Fulfill the law through love of course,
Desire fairness, but bless, don't curse.
be kind to all, leave wrath to the Lord,
and remember God will have the last word.

"All bitterness, fury, anger, shouting, and reviling must be removed from you, along with all malice. Be kind to one another, compassionate, forgiving one another as God has forgiven you in Christ." (Ephesians 4:31-32 NAB)

"For I am in a strait betwixt two, having a desire to depart, and to be with Christ; which is far better: Nevertheless to abide in the flesh is more needful for you." (Philippians 1:23-24 KJV)

"I thank God through Jesus Christ our Lord. So then with the mind I myself serve the law of God; but with the flesh the law of sin." (Romans 7:25 KJV)

"Do I not hate, LORD, those who hate you? Those who rise against you, do I not loathe? With fierce hatred I hate them, enemies I count as my own." (Psalm 139:21-22 NAB)

"Yet there is no man on earth so just as to do good and never sin." (Ecclesiastes 7:20 NAB)

"I know your works, your labor, and your endurance, and that you cannot tolerate the wicked; you have tested those who call themselves apostles but are not, and discovered that they are impostors. Moreover, you have endurance and have suffered for my name, and you have not grown weary."

(Revelation 2:2-3 NAB)

"As it is written: 'There is no one just, not one, there is no one who understands, there is no one who seeks God. All have gone astray; all alike are worthless; there is not one who does good, (there is not) even one."(Romans 3:10-12 NAB)

"But now the righteousness of God has been manifested apart from the law, though testified to by the law and the prophets, the righteousness of God through faith in Jesus Christ for all who believe. For there is no distinction; all have sinned and are deprived of the glory of God." (Romans 3:21-23 NAB)

We Are Sore

Although Your return is forever nearer
It is still hard to be such bearers
To know Your love and share it with others
When people don't care or wish to be bothered.
When we think now about it we clearly see
That our souls yearn for Eternity.
We're sick of the hate, the doubt, and sorrow,
O come, our Lord, before tomorrow.
Please show all peoples the devil's face
Then take us to Your holy place.

To show the truth by telling Your story,
we wish to reveal to them Your glory.
And yet they laugh and still they mock
They joke around like it's a crock.
They kick dirt in our faces, make jokes and laugh,
But if it weren't for our faith, they'd feel *our* wrath.
What should we do? Forgive and forget?
How can we? people, whose minds have been set,
On drilling the truth into those that doubt
Your love that no one can live without.
You've already died and have risen again

By that You've conquered death and sin.
But people are still so very bad
And getting worse which makes us mad.
Our hearts feel as though they're in a vice
O God, when will you bring paradise?

Only You can be so kind
To those who do not seek to find
The Truth, the Love, the meaning of Life:
The things that soothe all of our strife.
Lord, it's hard; we can't take much more,
Each wrong we see makes us sore…

We pray each day we don't lose control,
That would be foolish, we'd lose our souls.
But often at times we think to give up
And join the crowd and live it up.
Then realizing again what's really right,
we pick up our heads, ready to fight.
It's awful, you see, if vengeance is sought,
It belongs to Him, because we've been bought,
By a ransom of blood poured out from His Son,
Our Savior the Christ that many still shun.

But if we lost all control our zeal would not quit
Until we knew that our last hit
Had ended the lives of men so cruel,
Whose jeers and doubts made us fools.
From those we'd love to rip out their throats

Drown them slowly and watch them float,
Or maybe impale them on a rusty stake
And send them to Hell so they can bake.
Their sins are so evil, so selfish, so vile,
Their acts bring to mind the taste of bile.

But wait just a minute, I don't understand…
If "saints" are kind throughout the land,
How can they kill and want to destroy?
Aren't they peaceful and prone to joy?
See the truth: that we're full of sin.
These terrors do lurk in the hearts of ALL men!
Not one of us is innocent…
To Hell we all deserve to be sent.

So remove this anger, it poisons the soul,
Purify us, O Lord, make us whole.
Alas it is not anyone's place to judge,
But with our knowledge we must try to budge
Stubborn thinking and evil ways
Towards the light of truth in these dark days.
By grace we are cleansed and born anew
Crucifying the flesh, placing all in You.

We must forgive and trust that He
Will come with justice and set us free.
Heaven on Earth, You've promised us, Lord
Saints know You'll come, we trust Your Word.
You'll send the Enemy to the Lake of Fire,

And all will see that there is no higher.
The world will be washed of all its hate
And the faithful will feel so very great.
But we fear for those whom we loved before
If they don't believe now and forevermore,
They'll die and never be risen again
To the life where we dwell in Your garden.
They'll all be forgotten, oblivious to us,
Who will live in peace without any fuss.
But we can't bear it now to think of that
The ones we love now won't be there to chat,
They'll be gone forever and ever more
But Thy will be done, Lord, and for now we are sore.

† † †

"Cast all your worries upon him because he cares for you. Be sober and vigilant. Your opponent the devil is prowling around like a roaring lion looking for (someone) to devour. Resist him, steadfast in faith, knowing that your fellow believers throughout the world undergo the same sufferings. The God of all grace who called you to his eternal glory through Christ (Jesus) will himself restore, confirm, strengthen, and establish you after you have suffered a little." (1 Peter 5:7-10 NAB)

"Similarly, these dreamers nevertheless also defile the flesh, scorn lordship, and revile glorious beings. Yet the archangel Michael, when he argued with the devil in a dispute over the body of Moses, did not venture to pronounce a reviling judgment upon him but said, "May the Lord rebuke you!" (Jude 1:8-9 NAB)

Uncompromising Vanity

The dragon stands proudly before the gates,
making claim to the Throne while wielding hellish fire,
commanding his deceived minions against the heavenly host
Throughout the cosmos a mighty roar thunders. MICHAEL!
Awakening a multitude of heavenly warriors,
the battle cry of angels summons the faithful
to the Glorified Presence.
Armed with swords of flashing lightning,
flying swiftly on immense wings,
they rise to defend the Eternal Light.
Led by the great prince,
the devoted servants swarm the legions of darkness.

The dragon is bound with adamant chains,
brought before the foot of the One
where he is overwhelmed by compassion
and a Will so transcendent, he is broken to the point of submission.
The dragon burns in torment for his foolish challenge,
consumed by arrogance and lust for power,
forgiveness for himself *by* himself is impossible.
So how could he ever seek absolution from the Creator he defied?
There's no other choice but to cast him from the skies.
The dragon must hide his shame and be sentenced,
existing full of hatred in exile forever.

"Pray without ceasing." (1 Thessalonians 5:17 NAB)

"Against you alone have I sinned; I have done such evil in your sight that you are just in your sentence, blameless when you condemn." (Psalms 51:6 NAB)

"If we acknowledge our sins, he is faithful and just and will forgive our sins and cleanse us from every wrongdoing." (1 John 1:9 NAB)

Confession

Do not ignore temptation or your pride like the one who has fallen,
Be mindful of your vices and on God always be calling,
And when you stray, don't hesitate; drop to your knees crawling.

Sins do not seem sinful, even when you know it's wrong.
Justified by reasoning, you just try to get along,
But nothing fools the Master who sees the weak as strong.

Examine your conscience well being sure nothing is omitted,
And upon honest revelation of the evil you committed,
Don't wait to confess in prayer the guilt you have admitted.

When we are quite alone, God comes to us for certain,
But so does the devil because he knows that we are hurting
Be on guard in constant prayer or be with disaster flirting.

Do not fault the devil, though he's been evil from the start,
Always seek forgiveness and let grace work in your heart.
Pray endlessly for protection, and God's Spirit will never part.

† † †

"I can do all things through Christ which strengtheneth me." (Philippians 4:13 KJV)

"and, like living stones, let yourselves be built into a spiritual house to be a holy priesthood to offer spiritual sacrifices acceptable to God through Jesus Christ." (1 Peter 2:5 NAB)

"He must increase; I must decrease." (John 3:30 NAB)

Less of me and more of Him

I have a goal in mind… challenging and rewarding.
I CAN AND I WILL…by the grace of God.

Many complications block my progress… difficult but manageable.
I can, and I WILL… by the grace of God.

Many obstacles hinder my actions… overwhelming and opposing.
I can, and I will… by the grace of God.

Many setbacks defeat my purpose… depressing and devastating.
I think I can, but will I?… by the grace of God.

Many mountains have risen up… immense and impossible.
I can't, but We will… by the grace of God.

The greatest victory has been accomplished… certain and enduring.
I could never but He did… BY THE GRACE OF GOD.

All or None

A neuron fires all or none,

Likewise, may it all be done.

Give wholly and freely, or not at all,

Intently listen to your call.

With love complete, yet never blind

Have genuine thoughts, simple and kind.

Hope for Heaven at the gates of hell,

And have faith in God, His might and will.

Endure with courage in the depths of fear,

Knowing His benevolent grace is near.

With every breath, then thank the Lord,

Finding true peace within the Word.

† † †

"Can any of you by worrying add a single moment to your life span?" (Matthew 6:27 NAB)

"Let no one deceive himself. If any one among you considers himself wise in this age, let him become a fool so as to become wise. For the wisdom of this world is foolishness in the eyes of God, for it is written: 'He catches the wise in their own ruses,' and again: 'The Lord knows the thoughts of the wise, that they are vain." (1 Corinthians 3:18-20 NAB)

"But rather, love your enemies and do good to them, and lend expecting nothing back; then your reward will be great and you will be children of the Most High, for he himself is kind to the ungrateful and the wicked." (Luke 6:35 NAB)

Fatherly Advice

A thoughtful observant man once told me:
People have short memories of good times.
Your kindnesses are easily forgotten,
yet your shortcomings are etched in stone.
Their selfishness will dismiss your needs for their own sake.
Take care of yourself.

A judicious practical man once offered this advice:
When it comes to others, do what is in your best interest.
Your kindnesses are self-serving and rewarding,
and your shortcomings are life-lessons.
Take care of yourself…

Even a wise ancient man once taught me:
Fulfillment comes from selflessness and sacrifice.
What is in your best interest should be the wellness of others.
Your kindnesses serve others,
and your response to shortcomings are models of behavior.
Take care of yourself to take care of others…

Fatherly Advice

A graceful benevolent spirit once moved me:
Success comes to fruition through faith and persistence.
Helpers are always near and provide assistance as needed.
You are never alone, therefore do not falter.
Be slow to anger and reluctant to retaliate.
Be gracious, be kind, and when they hurt you,
Live blessed and love on them anyway...
For with faith by grace, you are taken care of already.

† † †

"I am your servant; give me discernment that I may understand your statutes." (Psalm 119:125 KJV)

"Just so, every good tree bears good fruit, and a rotten tree bears bad fruit. A good tree cannot bear bad fruit, nor can a rotten tree bear good fruit. Every tree that does not bear good fruit will be cut down and thrown into the fire. So by their fruits you will know them." (Matthew 7:17-20 NAB)

"Enter ye in at the strait gate: for wide is the gate, and broad is the way, that leadeth to destruction, and many there be which go in thereat: Because strait is the gate, and narrow is the way, which leadeth unto life, and few there be that find it." (Matthew 7:13-14 KJV)

"Trust in the Lord with all your heart, on your own intelligence rely not; in all your ways be mindful of him, and he will make straight your paths." (Proverbs 3:5-6 NAB)

Discernment

Have I been betrayed…? By another or by my own perceptions?

It was just a dream. Which part is the lie? Then or Now?
Foolish illusion, I see it now, revealed by its actions.
I saw it once, bathed in light. I felt it once, wrapped in warmth.
It was just a glare in my eye, an emotion in my body.

I see it now, but it's draped in shadow. I feel it no more. Betrayed.
Just a demon in disguise sent to test me… ??

Was I betrayed…? By another's choices or by my own innocence?

It is never a dream. Our lives are real, full of experience.
No illusions, only changes in awareness for surmised reasons and unclear purposes.
Meditation through time, contemplation through prayer, and understanding through revelations all impart wisdom.
Why we must undergo such demoralizing trials is granted in time,
Always in His time.

I see it now, clarified by faith. I feel it again, shielded in belief.
Just an angel in view sent to redirect me to the strait and narrow…

† † †

"Brothers, I for my part do not consider myself to have taken possession. Just one thing: forgetting what lies behind but straining forward to what lies ahead, I continue my pursuit toward the goal, the prize of God's upward calling, in Christ Jesus." (Philippians 3:13-14 NAB)

"Then he said to his disciples, 'The harvest is abundant but the laborers are few; so ask the master of the harvest to send out laborers for his harvest." (Mathew 9:37-38 NAB)

Some Bridges must be Burned

What's done is done, stop looking back
The match has been lit.
Forgiveness cuts the links,
But if you hold the chain, then you're still bound…

What's done is done, stop looking back
The flames have caught ablaze.
Be renewed, be refined,
the bridge behind must burn.
He calls you forward, you must come alone…
Then…Then, He'll send you out to assemble those in disrepair.

What's done is done; there's no way back…
And so you are sent…
There's much to do and less time to do it,
There is much to gain, but few to gather.

What's done is done, and what wills will be.
Press on toward the mark,
The goal will always be in sight
When the Cause is in your heart.

The Mystery of Love…

"We love because he first loved us." (1John 4:19 NAB)

"Love is patient. Love is kind. It is not jealous, is not pompous, it does not seek its own interests, it is not quick-tempered, it does not brood over injury, it does not rejoice over wrongdoing but rejoices with the truth. It bears all things, believes all things, hopes all things, endures all things. Love never fails…" (1 Corinthians 13:4-8 NAB)

From what I understand, love is not born immortal. It does not come to be or develop from nothing. It is an everlasting bond between Creator and creation and among blessed creatures. Mysteriously though, as unchanging as that appears, it seems to live, and therefore, move and grow with experience. But no matter how you look at it, love truly is a mystery. It is probably considered to be among the highest of virtues by every kind of person. Paradoxically, while it can bring the greatest joys to someone, it can simultaneously cause the worst agony and stress. It is the most frequent theme in literature and more songs and poems have been written to capture its splendor than any other ideal. Likewise, its inevitable loss within time is also the ultimate idea causing the epitome of anguish. This is even in spite of faith in love's eternal endurance. And so I repeat that love is a great mystery of life.

People often describe love in a relationship as a "give and take," "a two-way street." I disagree. From what I understand of love as it is described throughout the Bible and in my own experiences, there is no give and take, just give. Love is a one-way street issued from the heart toward the object of that love. That giver doesn't then look to take from the object of his/her affection, but rather is open to receive the same love coming down a separate one-way street from someone else who has been blessed with the same godly attribute. One can hope to receive love back from its object, but not selfishly expect it as a conditional result of its demonstration. Hope is a virtue then in the sense that one may and will hope for the return of affection, but it need not be looked forward to greedily. In that way, when love is shared mutually between partners, ideally in a true marriage, love is a reciprocal thing since the hope of the continual sharing of love is present along with the actual expression of it.

So, you might say to yourself, "Well, aren't two one-way streets in opposite directions the same thing as a two-way street of give and take?" Not quite. Allow me to elaborate. Real love happens without expectation not only of reward but of recognition as well. It is an entity that requires no external feedback to assure itself of its own goodness. It is sincere self-sacrifice. Therefore, it has the unique ability to sustain itself on its own joy (so long as its *source* is genuine, which ultimately is a gift from God).

When love drives down this street from the heart in the carpool lane with expectation of any kind, it sets itself up for a head-on collision with disappointment. If not that, it is ready to get off at the nearest exit toward a different destination. Either way, this love does not stay on the right path driving toward its object freely and selflessly, carrying with it many blessings.

We must keep in mind also that, more often than not, the object of love is another human being. Since humans are extremely fallible, loving any one of them with expectations of an equal "give and take" mentality is absurd. It is selfish to love someone or claim to love someone when those actions of love are based on the reasoning: "If I show love to this individual, then I will get it back from him/her." This conditional love can only result in frequent disappointment when the object of affection fails to return the sentiments in the *expected* manner. This love is uncertain and also tends to lead to another condition: "If/when I don't get love back, I will cease giving it." Clearly, this is selfish and not real love.

Another problem that arises with a frequent lack of return is the development of a type of learned helplessness. Essentially, people without deeply rooted faith in God will likely give up on others and withdraw inwardly. The expression of love becomes difficult and emotionally exhausting, causing a complete lack of trust in any individual outside one's own closest circle of confidants. This could lead to a rather lonesome existence. I know I'm guilty of this from time to time; are you?

These types of situations are also compounded by the variable of communication. If this kind of love is a street with expectation nagging the driver, and if the driver is unaware that the other car doesn't see him/her coming, then a disaster is about to take place. I would be remiss if I didn't insert my thoughts here about how misperceptions of a situation can cause people to veer off the right road completely. Apparently, unless the streets of communication are smooth, open, without cracks or traffic jams, and frequently mended, then misperceptions are inevitable. Sometimes a lack of communication regarding expectations is enough to cause the *feelings* accompanying a conditional love to change, thereby giving the person a perception that the situation is not favorable or desired. When these feelings change, it is likely that a person will follow them down another road, which unfortunately leads to a lot of heartache.

In any case, conditions of any kind for actions of love other than the sake of love itself have selfish motivations. In my mind then, the above scenarios are not the same as real love. I hope you can see that the type described above is fairly common in society and tremendously based on perception. Perception is simply a fancy word for feeling and/or emotion, which are determined naturally on a person's experience of situations related to the feelings/emotions of love and its effects. Consequently, they are extremely susceptible to change in reaction or response to changing circumstances. This makes love in the world a fleeting thing, a careless and carefree passion. It causes much pain and suffering to those who give and then don't receive because they had an expectation that was not fulfilled. These disappointments occur within children and adults alike from neglect or misunderstanding and are perpetuated throughout a lifetime by subsequent choices in response to similar disappointing circumstances.

On the other hand, if the perfection of God is admitted into the equation, then real love is not the everyday emotion that many experience. Rather, Love is a subtle, yet powerful force that is not swayed by circumstance. Accordingly, I cannot conceive of a loving God being so fickle in His treatment of His beloved creation. Questions that arise here would be the age old: "well if God loves us, why do good people suffer?" and "how can there be a hell if God loves us?" Well, certainly anyone of faith would turn to scripture for answers to these troublesome queries. Ones that give me understanding are listed among the poems written in this section as well as the previous one. Proverbs, Psalms, and Ecclesiastes surely contain several truths that explain God's intentions (as if He needs to answer to you). Additionally, there are numerous passages in the Gospels and explanations in the letters of Paul about God's unfathomable love for His creation. Furthermore, the great love story of the entire Bible taken as a whole is a testament to God's merciful patience with His disobedient creatures, which cause the suffering in the first place. For indeed, we don't give love back to God properly the way we're supposed to all the time. Many books have been written on this subject, so I don't want to reinvent the wheel. When you have the Spirit and willingness to, go read the Bible yourself and the thousands of commentaries about God's merciful love for you. Why, even now is a good time to put this book down and go read the third chapter in the Gospel of John, fifty third in Isaiah, and the fifth chapter in the Letter to the Romans (to start).

† † †

Anyways, choice seems to be a large part of how we behave in most situations. I could ramble and argue about the effects of our choices on those around us for several pages, but I feel I've done that already in my first book. So, before I go too far down a tangent, I must return to the idea of how steadfast and limitless God's love is for us.

When I read through 1Corinthians 13:4-8, I tend to believe that real love is unchanging in its purpose and effects unlike the selfish love described previously. Here, the apostle Paul says what love is and what love is not. As you read over those poetic verses at the beginning of this chapter, you should be able to clearly see the unchanging nature of love. The verses don't say or even hint at the notion of love being patient *sometimes* or kind *only if a person is kind in return.* Love doesn't *occasionally hold grudges* just in case its pain can be used later to get what it wants from a person. There is no reading between the lines or fine print. Love doesn't enter into serious commitments and back out of them for any circumstance or excuse. No, *real* love hopes and endures and *never* fails. Ignorance, pride, fear, immaturity (and others)... these are the traits of men and women that cause the appearance of love to fail. However, God's message of love throughout the Bible doesn't say that love fails *once in a while* or even that it *can* fail. The bold statement is absolute: it *never* fails. Logically, I am led to believe (if I am to believe and have faith in Him) that if something does seem to fail, it wasn't because love failed, but it's because something else was the root of the situation and our foolish human choices interfered with the expression of the dedicated nature of real love.

However, I declare that even apparent failures and devastating disappointments can be overcome when approached with real love, thereby keeping its undefeated streak alive. When someone sins gravely against us or even when we gravely sin against others, (whether family member, spouse, friend, co-worker, or organization) the human tendency is to react negatively to the responsible party with: anger, vengeance, or bitterness. He, she, or, it becomes the enemy. Human understanding and logic says that "justice" must be done and punishment served to that individual or group for his/her/its crime against us. They deserve to suffer. Yet, that only causes a transgression from you to the other party. How silly to perpetuate such madness. Jesus said to *love* our enemies, not to repay blow for blow. Saints are called, no, *commanded* to love. As a result, having love for the vehicle of our suffering leads to forgiveness. Forgiveness is a liberating action for both the transgressor and the one trespassed against. Such a divine condition can only exist with real selfless love. It results in the surrender of all desire for retribution. In spite of personal tragedy, a saint is asked (in faith) to deny this so utterly basic human desire for personal justice. The satisfaction of the self and its desperate thirst for it are abandoned in the presence of real love. After hearing stories of pain and suffering, and even as I have been experiencing a sizeable load of emotional and spiritual pain within myself, the execution of such a complete act of submission truly requires divine intervention. This divine condition requires a choice that will allow that intercession to occur. When I look around, this appears to be a rare, special, powerful gift indeed, and I have been searching and praying for it constantly. Fortunately, as I have mentioned before, I know that by faith, God grants this gift completely in time, and so faith gives rise to a hope that I am being (and therefore anyone can be) given the grace for the strength to always choose peace over anger, forgiveness over revenge, and love over bitterness.

And so, it is for these reasons that as far as I am concerned, love is no mere feeling. My advice to my readers is if you find yourself basing your decisions in the realm of committed relationships on your feelings (whether it is a spouse, a job, an ideal, or some other vocation), I warn you that you may be playing with fire, and you may want to reevaluate your situation. If you are already in a situation that requires a true self-sacrificing love and you are thinking of backing out because it doesn't "feel good," DON'T! Pray instead. Put your whole faith in God and ask for the tools necessary to succeed, and you will succeed. For if you base every decision on mere feelings, your life is going to be a tumultuous pattern of events. You should realize that your feelings toward various things are highly influenced by circumstance and experience and constantly subject to change. If not, then please take my word for it. For a simple example though, think about a song that you may absolutely rave about when you first hear it, but then it loses its impact after the thousandth time it is played on the radio in less than a month. Even still, after not hearing it for several years, you may have positive feelings toward it once more when you play it again or hear it randomly. It might remind you of a simpler or more enjoyable time. Whatever the reason, time alters your perception of it.

On the other hand, certain foods or drinks may be unpalatable the first time you try them, but there would not be such a thing as an "acquired taste" if people did not change their attitudes and feelings. Would you be willing to say you "love" some of these inanimate things? If so, it's not a real love, just a temporal fondness.

Now, these two examples are relatively trivial matters. Sadly though, many people treat others and real love in the same manner. Real love is a choice, a decision to surrender the self for the service and well-being of its object. And if you choose to love something one day, you must make the same choice the next day. This only happens and *can* only happen with God in your heart. He is the source of real love, He showed us the way, and commands us to remain in Him to have that source of love in us pouring forth like a fountain, welling up within. It is this real love that is so easily exploited by the world because its nature is to continue giving regardless of hardship or mistreatment. Mercifully, love is coupled with faith and given hope to endure such trials with the understanding that we *can* endure because "God first loves us." So whenever the elements of the world interfere, saints do rest assured in the truth that God most definitely loves them, thereby sustaining them. Given that reality, saints are granted sufficient grace to love genuinely in spite of ephemeral emotions, wavering attitudes, and unpredictable circumstances.

† † †

So why would an omnipotent God love us anyway? Saints seem so adamantly confident that God loves them. And anytime someone says something seemingly profound or important confidently, we tend to take for granted why he or she is saying it so factually. How often do you accept something just because an authority figure or so-called expert says so? Strictly rational thinkers base most of their decisions and essentially their beliefs on things that can be physically or at least logically proven. I certainly was led to the truths of Christianity by this approach, though ultimately the certitude in my heart is absolutely a matter of faith.

I have commented a bit on the human understanding of love. So, now I will feebly attempt to describe (yet fall tremendously short) the other side: the inexhaustible incomprehensible love of God. Out of love, seeing that His creation was good, God created mankind. And after we were able to become aware of ourselves, we chose to "love" ourselves more than God, which delivered us to death. The result, enacted by our choice of disobedience, is a separation from God and causes all suffering. In His foreknowledge, God designs a plan of redemption… why? Simple: love!

To boil down the Gospel message, you (me and everyone else too) have sinned and are apart from the Creator. Sin causes such a blemish; it's like that stubborn stain on your favorite shirt that just won't come out. Bleach and stain removers just discolor the fabric, and frequent washing just makes the color around it fade. No matter how much you scrub or various chemicals you use on it, it just won't come out. And when you are invited to a wonderful banquet, how many of you would wear a stained shirt to the reception? Or, if you did, how many would be let in with it?

I hope none of you would want to wear a stained shirt to an extravagant event. Anyway, since you have no means to clean your stain no matter how much effort you exert or fancy things you use to hide it or wash it away, you are going to need a new one. This leaves three options. The first two are similar in that you must actively do something. That is, you could make a new shirt or buy one. Interestingly enough, if it is just you and your stained shirt, then you have nothing of value to purchase one and no materials to create a new one…

With any fortune, you're realizing that I'm not really talking about a shirt per se, but your soul. Jesus taught with parables, and the above situation is based directly on them, especially the ones that describe the Kingdom of God as a wedding banquet (Matthew 22:2). If you haven't made that connection, my analogy here makes absolutely no sense. Regardless, there are several philosophies out there both new age and ancient that would argue that you personally have the ability to both create for yourself a new clean soul or by mere exercise of will to remove the stain of innate negativity completely by your own efforts via meditation, special breathing practices, fasting, or other physical or mental action. The Gospel (which in case you are unaware, means good news) says that's not an option. The only other way then to get a new shirt is to be given one. Salvation then is a gift, one of grace by the mercy and love of God. The question then becomes: how is that received?

Well, here is the really good news: God loves you. To prove it, He qualifies love in scripture as self-sacrifice. So, recognizing that

His fallen creation is incapable of redeeming itself, seeing that it is broken, weak, just a fragile vapor, He comes down from Heaven. Giving up the eternal majesty of His divinity and power, He takes on the form of crude flesh in the humblest of circumstances. As He walks and talks as one of us proclaiming His love, without objection, He then bears the burden and punishment for all our sins, i.e. in a most excruciatingly painful death: crucifixion.

† † †

Here's another thought that has crossed my mind. So many people are angry at God for their lots in life. They dare to curse Him, ignore Him, and blame Him for all the evil in the world, even go as far to say that He doesn't even exist. Okay, I guess that's "fair" from the human perspective. And using that perception for the sake of this case, God understands it. And so, I see the following rationale within the life, death, and resurrection of Jesus. God says, "We created man and gave him choice which led to evil, death and suffering. It's only fitting then if We receive the punishment for being ultimately responsible. So if by Our law, death is the wage for sin, We must sacrifice Ourselves for their sake and save them from themselves and from Our justified wrath." Now, I certainly cannot claim to "know the mind of God," that would probably be blasphemous. I would rather say that by faith I can see the logic in the message despite the illogical grace and mystery at its core. For those of you who think God doesn't care, and you want to curse Him for your troubles, I hope you understand that you already have. You have whipped Him mercilessly, crowned Him mockingly with thorns, hammered your nails into His breaking body, spat and ridiculed Him for His abundant grace. Every lie, every act of greed, lust, denial, etc. all make the Creator weep for you. So He washes you clean by the blood of His self-sacrifice as payment for the soul's redemptive work you are fundamentally incapable of doing. Accept that *truth*, admit the responsibility of your immoral actions and necessity of redemption, i.e. give up your self-pride, and you will be reunited with God, and His Holy Spirit will work wonders in your heart.

It seems counterintuitive I know, given the fact the world says you can do anything you set your mind to. Just look into your own life though at the many simple things you've let yourself down with when trying to accomplish them by yourself. It's insanity to me to think that anyone can believe that he or she has the ability to achieve a gift as incredible as eternal life by something he or she does in this short, physically limited life. Perhaps that's not your goal; maybe you have no fear of death or the unknown that awaits you afterward, or maybe you just haven't considered it yet. I think it's worth investigating before you get too old or embittered to care anything about it. Even the most intellectually talented should become aware at some point that they are entirely incapable of knowing and doing everything for themselves (yet another topic I elaborate on in my previous work).

Upon recognizing your need of God's mercy through the sacrifice of His Son Jesus, you will want to get rid of all the sin causing you so much pain, guilt and shame in the light of His love. It takes a little action on your part, but be consoled that the Holy Spirit is prompting it and carrying you through it: repent. Repent by confessing your sin out loud to God and in faith know God hears your cries. Peace will be given to you as God forgives you of your sins. Only love can allow that. Once this grace is received as a gift of the love of God for you, life and the world really does take on a new meaning. You are liberated, free to love and forgive others as well, including a genuine love for your self and your inherent worth as an adopted child of the living God.

And when God forgives, it's not like a human accepting an apology superficially and then holding onto memories of the sin to perhaps use as a weapon against the individual later. No, true forgiveness, like that from God, is far more complete. According to many verses, some in Psalm 103 especially, we see God's immense love dealing with us not as we deserve, but rather out of love, His mercy endures with patience as He calls us home to Him one by one. Sadly, given the free gift of love, it must be freely received, and some people will continuously reject the offer and end up permanently separated from God. This serves as the foundation for the idea that God does not send people to hell, but individuals walk freely into it by following their own paths away from God. For without the freedom to accept an alternative, love and eternal life is not a gift.

Interestingly, the Bible also describes Christ's crucifixion, the greatest act of mercy and grace, as foolishness in 1 Corinthians 1:17-31. Check that out; it's quite a string of verses that brings the reality of human arrogance to mind. Think about the gift of God's salvation again in terms of your stained shirt. If someone bought you a new shirt and gave it to you as a gift (for no reason other than that the person loves you)… would you take it, say "thank you," and then stuff it in a drawer? Put it on and show it off? Or say, "No thanks, I have my own shirt, or will go get my own?" God offers each of us eternal life with Him if we but believe in His Son who suffered and died in our place, essentially telling each of us, "take it or leave it." I pray you take it and become one of His saints.

What's more, who or what are we that we even pass into the mind of God (Psalm 8:3-4 KJV)? And yet not only is He mindful of each of us, He knows us so intimately and loves us regardless (Matthew 6:26; Luke 12:6-7). Such sentiments are sung about in the Psalms and throughout the New Testament. If you're lacking this love that is so pure, put down this book for a while and open God's love letter to you. If you feel like you aren't ready yet, then keep reading; I have much more to share in the final poems of this book to strengthen your faith or penetrate your doubts.

† † †

Interestingly, when I step out of my believer's mindset and read the words above as a skeptic, the psychologist in me attempts to diagnose the negative self-image as some sort of inherent low self-esteem of Christians. Saints apparently think so poorly of themselves and the human race in general. No wonder you see a bunch of low-life bums saying they "found Jesus" just seemingly to avoid the effects of crimes or serious vices, but that's not for a "good person like me." I understand the thought process, but pray the deception that isolates with this pride is removed that those of you who think that way may reconnect to the source of life itself. One must be humbled before the awesome holiness of God before one is ready to receive such a gift. For with the realization of our own brokenness by the grace of God, we are enlightened to the truth of what each of us was intended to be: a beloved child of God. A saint is not depressed, self-defeating, nor prone to thinking lowly of his or her self-worth. No, on the contrary, a saint is filled with the spirit of knowing they are a blessed and precious child, embraced by the love of God. And so, saints are called to rejoice in all circumstances, good or bad, giving thanks to God through the savior Jesus.

Upon further reflection, I imagine what some people will think after reading the last few paragraphs. Indeed, the phrase "easier said than done" comes to mind. Although some of my ideas can be idealistic, the reality of the experience of God's love working in my life is evident to me. The ideal of pressing on through the most difficult times because of love is not impossible, but actually quite practical and fulfilling. During the most intense and troublesome times of my trial, my emotional and spiritual torture was physically compounded by a sudden loss of fifteen pounds, (mostly due to lack of appetite and eating), a compressed cervical disk that caused severe neck and back pain, and an excruciating tooth abscess that resulted eventually in a root canal. Meanwhile, I had to keep my personal life in the background so I could tend to my professional duties, which mainly dealt with junior high and high school nonsense. Frustrating students refusing to follow simple assignment instructions and ridiculous "problems" like "so and so took my pencil" were almost enough to walk straight out the door in light of the issues I had to face outside of work.

However, prayer focused my attention on the bigger picture and kept my mind fixed on the deeper purpose of my presence as a teacher. Because of love, for God mostly, and by extension, for the students themselves, I was given the grace to continue one day at a time. Granted, my spirit was not the most productive, energetic, or pleasant to be around all the time, I was given a great understanding to do my job proficiently with patience and able to grow in my role as a leader in the classroom.

As I prayed throughout that time, there were many signs that allowed me to accept the reality of my situation despite my learned instinct to cling to apparently hollow promises and empty words from the past. I was often reminded in scriptures that actions do speak louder than words. Also, whenever I asked "why?" no matter about what, whether it was why this trial came to me, why my toothache was driving me insane, or why my eighth graders wouldn't stop talking, I was "randomly" answered by a number of different sources, and I quote: "that's just the way it is." It was during these horrible times when I wanted to throw in the towel, abandon my career, fall asleep and wake up somewhere else as someone else. After a summer reliving everything in my relationship from start to finish, wondering over and over if I had been doing the right thing and beginning to compile my poems and thoughts, I opened up my Bible to First Timothy chapter 4 and read: "Do not neglect the gift you have, which was conferred on you through the prophetic word with the imposition of hands of the presbyterate. Be diligent in these matters, be absorbed in them, so that your progress may be evident to everyone. Attend to yourself and to your teaching; persevere in both tasks, for by doing so you will save both yourself and those who listen to you" (1 Timothy 4:14-16 NAB).

I began to let go of my past more in faith and within a few weeks began a new school year with a far more optimistic attitude and a new class to teach: New Testament Theology. Again, I was faced with a difficult schedule with a challenging set of students, and often times when my frustration with them manifested, I was asked, "why do you teach then?" It is an automatic response now to point up toward the crucifix that hangs in every classroom, and I tell them, "It would be worse if I didn't get upset when you don't meet the expectation. It would be worse if I didn't respond to the lack of performance that occurs from time to time. Indifference is a cruel poison." So, how can anyone explain sacrificing so much for the sake of others? It's simple. Love. I love teaching because I love God. I love God because that's how He made me. I do my best for love of Him, and when I slack off because I'm still just a man, then I get upset and ask for more strength, more understanding, more compassion, more, more, more. And the love He has for me according to the faith is all that is necessary to motivate me and anyone for that matter to endure the difficulties of life and its chances in all their forms. When I first began to write poetry back in high school, I kept it to myself. The words were my expressions, for me, and me alone. How silly to keep such a gift to oneself. After maturing in faith a bit over the past ten to thirteen years, I have come to realize that love allows and calls for much more self-sacrifice and sharing. As I handled my professional duties with more grace than before, I applied my other writing gifts and worked many late hours throughout the year on this manuscript with the intention of sharing it with many for the "building up of the body of Christ" (Ephesians 4:12 NAB).

† † †

At this point, I believe I have verbalized enough about love to give you some things to think about. It is difficult to express to those who are unwilling to receive it or give it in return. The love from God is incomprehensible, indescribable, and inexplicable. He just does, or should I say, "that's just the way it is." This is a fact of faith that someone of faith cannot be persuaded to think otherwise. It is so overwhelming to try and wrap our limited minds around it. So, I suppose if you are to take any piece of advice from this reflection on love, it is that real love is a wonderful thing: so very precious and so very powerful. Cling to real love when you seem to find it or find occasion to share it. Cherish one another always in all circumstances, for not only is it the way of saints, but it's the way and commandment of God. Finally, while love can at times seem to be an extraordinarily simple thing, for our own shortcomings, we can make it a perplexing obsession. I began this chapter twice saying a truth about love, and so for the sense of completeness, I'll say it a third time: undoubtedly, love is a mystery. Enjoy the following streams that cascaded from my mind in response to love's meditations…

"But grace was given to each of us according to the measure of Christ's gift."
(Ephesians 4:7 NAB)

"You belong to God, children, and you have conquered them, for the one who is in you is greater than the one who is in the world.
(1 John 4:4 NAB)"

Do you hear that… There it is again…
Don't you hear that sound coming from within?

God graces each of us with certain gifts, talents, powers,
And surrounds us all with awesome sights, beasts, and flowers.
We all are granted so many things; his wonders never cease,
But the one that troubles me right now is the topic of this piece.
The universe seems infinitely large, for nothing can contain his love,
But what's bestowed in us differs from that which is from above.

Do you hear that… There it is again…
Don't you hear that sound coming from within?

He put as many gifts as He could into each and every soul,
So that they'd be ready to go out and fill their special roles.
Some have wisdom, some have kindness,
Some are faithful and some are pious.
All have their fill of things which help them get along
But the gift of love that everyone gets is why I write this song.

Do you hear that… There it is again…
Don't you hear that sound coming from within?

His love springs endlessly and so needs no regeneration,
But the love that dwells inside of us is of a simpler creation.
The love we have is to be shared with all of those we meet,
And the kind of love existing in friends is nothing that can be beat.
But our little selves have limited space and so can't forever give
Without being loved in return by them, we're likely not to live.

Do you hear that… There it is again…
Don't you hear that sound coming from within?

It is taught to love everyone, expecting nothing in return,
But a problem lies in this selfless act, a lesson we must learn…
Our love is not like that above, which pours without an end,
Because we're full, then give some away to family or a friend.
Most often than not, it is mutually shared between cherished ones,
but sometimes we find nothing coming back and slowly out it runs.

Do you hear that… There it is again…
Don't you hear that sound coming from within?

When someone gives of themselves, but doesn't ever receive,
The love, which once was very strong, begins to take its leave.
The problem with the selfless loving spoken of before,
Is the feeling which arises when a person can give no more.
An isolated and lonely fog forms and clouds the mind
From those who normally loved them back and seemed so very kind.

Do you hear that… There it is again…
Don't you hear that sound coming from within?

A void, in the soul itself, manifests
Alone. The empty feeling like unwanted guests.
But this void can be filled, so no hope is lost,
And you can make it happen at such a little cost.
If ever you have felt this pain, then know you've been enticed
To open your heart fully to Jesus Lord our Christ…

Do you hear that… There it is again…
Don't you hear that sound coming from within?

That sound which resonates throughout these lines
Is the echoing of a void where our love usually shines…
Having never gotten solace in the world outside our minds,
Inside we must retreat, where we seek Him and we will find,
All the LOVE He has for us and the Faith to persevere,
Greater is He within us than the devil that lurks out there.

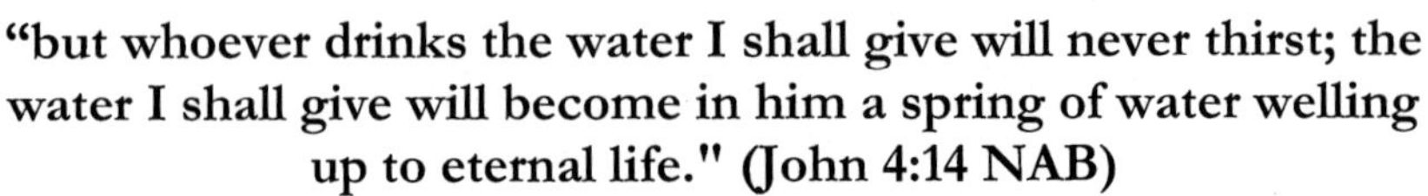
"but whoever drinks the water I shall give will never thirst; the water I shall give will become in him a spring of water welling up to eternal life." (John 4:14 NAB)

"I am the vine, you are the branches. Whoever remains in me and I in him will bear much fruit, because without me you can do nothing." (John 15:5 NAB)

"Behold, I am sending you like sheep in the midst of wolves; so be shrewd as serpents and simple as doves." (Matthew 10:16 NAB)

"I continue my pursuit toward the goal, the prize of God's upward calling, in Christ Jesus." (Philippians 3:14 NAB)

Do you hear that… a joyful tune sung from deep inside? Don't you hear that song from where His love abides?

Newly born and fashioned, we're adopted now by God,
Finding strength and comfort there in His staff and rod,
His endless love becomes a spring, emerging from our souls,
Able to carry us on and in faith fulfill our roles.
A new sound has taken form and joyfully it rings,
By the grace of God! The heart forever kindly sings.

Do you hear that… a joyful tune sung from deep inside?
Don't you hear that song from where His love abides?

No voiding echo, emptiness, or heartache to feel,
God's might will always shield us; His grace, a faithful seal.
The Risen Jesus smiles as he sits at the Father's side
Sending forth His Holy Spirit to always be our guide
And with mercy and forgiveness flowing freely from on high,
Faith will move us rightly, and we'll never question why.

Do you hear that… a joyful tune sung from deep inside?
Don't you hear that song from where His love abides?

Now rooted firmly in the vine, branches have been germinated,
Watered by God's love and with truth illuminated,
We must go out into the world, with its wolves and all its threats,
Preaching goodness to the lowly, forgiving them their debts.
So as gentle as the lamb and yet more cunning than the viper,
Although few are here to reap, the harvest won't be riper.

Do you hear that… a joyful tune sung from deep inside?
Don't you hear that song from where His love abides?

In any given moment God can use you for His glory,
So, study night and day, be prepared to share His story,
Be vigilant and cautious with never-ending prayers
Mindfully avoiding the devil and his snares.
Spread the Gospel with all kindness, and with eyes upon the prize,
Carry on until the end knowing in heaven your treasure lies.

† † †

"He was mindful that they were flesh, a breath that passes and does not return." (Psalm 78:39 NAB)

"You have no idea what your life will be like tomorrow. You are a puff of smoke that appears briefly and then disappears." (James 4:14 NAB)

"For he knows how we are formed; he remembers that we are dust. Man's days are like those of grass; like a flower of the field he blooms;"(Psalm 103:14-15 NAB)

Just A Precious Vapor

How odd.

Barely a droplet ourselves,
We pass through life, a mystified cloud
mostly ignoring the miracles of one another.
But on the brink of imminent loss,
after years have gone by in a flash,
Or perhaps the simple realization of our inevitable passing,
we see life for what it is:

a precious vapor

.

Here today, then gone before you know it.
Terminally ill patients, recovered addicts, repentant sinners
embrace true reality and revel in each experience like it was their first,
graciously giving thanks as if the last:

a precious vapor.

Meanwhile, the normal suffer obliviously
chasing worthless treasure, constantly moving toward the next selfish sensation.
If they could but see the gold in the hearts they ignore…
…especially their own.

precious vapors.

This life is too short for causing pain. Avoid making it.
Too short for anger and its greedy hunger. Dismiss it.
Bitterness restrains the soul. Give it up.
And with these weights lifted,
Let your precious vapor drift toward heaven
to be snatched from the winds of evil and time
to a peaceful eternity
as a fragrant aroma to the throne of God,
to be refreshed with grace and mercy,
inhaled deeply by the Creator with love.

Fragile, special, unique…
:::you:::
are such a precious vapor…

† † †

"They will throw them into the fiery furnace, where there will be wailing and grinding of teeth." (Matthew 13:42 NAB)

"Do not let your hearts be troubled. You have faith in God; have faith also in me. In my Father's house there are many dwelling places. If there were not, would I have told you that I am going to prepare a place for you?" (John 14:1-2 NAB)

Just Another Friend

Saints would hug to say goodbye,
And even hello, but you'd wonder: why?
You might not greet me with embrace
Nor approach me with a smiling face.
For I am Death, the dark Grim Reaper,
But definitely not a saint's final keeper.

It's shocking, perhaps, but certainly you'll find
Although seen as a beast, indeed I am kind.
Surely, your frightened view falls apart,
When doubt and fear have left your heart.
I have power to release you from guilt and pain
Freeing you finally forever from chains,
But only for **saints** is that my role
For to them I'm a messenger, bringing their soul
back to God where it belongs
Amidst the angels and their songs.

But if at death your sins are binding,
There will be wailing and teeth grinding.
Ominous foreboding on your last breath
Will only transmit your soul at death
Down to hell where it awaits
Torment, fire, and the worst of all fates.

So with faith in Christ, avoid this doom
in His Father's house, reserve a room,
And it's safe then to say that in the end
When you're a saint, I'm just another friend.

"For I am convinced that neither death, nor life, nor angels, nor principalities, nor present things, nor future things, nor powers, nor height, nor depth, nor any other creature will be able to separate us from the love of God in Christ Jesus our Lord." (Romans 8:38-39 NAB)

"But you, Lord, are a merciful and gracious God, slow to anger, most loving and true." (Psalm 86:15 NAB)

"It is of the LORD's mercies that we are not consumed, because his compassions fail not. They are new every morning: great is thy faithfulness." (Lamentations 3:22-23 KJV)

"The one who sat on the throne said, 'Behold, I make all things new…" (Revelation 21:5 NAB)

There's Not Enough

Another cold despite the shots?
Flu scares among the old and tots?
Identity stolen or totaled car?
Too many late nights at the bar?
Can't find work or been downsized?
Status falsely compromised?

Terror and war stealing youth?
"Friends" hiding and bending truth?
Tragic news of suicide?
Hearing that a friend has died?
Gambled away the rent for fun?
Death of daughter? Or maybe son?
Miscarriage bringing fears?
Stillbirth silence causing tears?
A cheating or deserting spouse?
In a fire, lost the house?
Divorce your only path to take?
Attending yet another wake?
Hurt again, arm in a sling?
Diagnosed with cancer's sting?
Unable to move from pain or age?
Needy burden rather than sage?

All of these are hard to touch,
And even one can be too much
For anybody to have to face
Without the strength of heavenly grace.

Imagine that it ***all*** befell you,
Know the comfort that I will tell you:
Simply put: ***there's not enough***!
Of pain or loss or evil stuff,
To keep God's LOVE from blessing you,
Rebuilding and making all things new.

† † †

"But God proves his love for us in that while we were still sinners Christ died for us." (Romans 5:8 NAB)

"Can a mother forget her infant, be without tenderness for the child of her womb? Even should she forget, I will never forget you." (Isaiah 49:15 NAB)

Cosmic Irony

He caught you when you fell down flat,
but you continued on to run.

He was there when you were crying,
but you were blinded by your tears.

He graced you with His wisdom,
but you ignored and went your way.

He loved you deep with mercy and peace,
but you turned away from Him.

He watched and waited patiently,
but you refused to turn around.

You always seem to hear His voice,
but you rarely choose to listen.

And you think you're all alone down here,
But He is the lonely one.

† † †

"Then said Jesus, 'Father, forgive them; for they know not what they do.' And they parted his raiment, and cast lots." (Luke 23:34 KJV)

"Then he fell to his knees and cried out in a loud voice, 'Lord, do not hold this sin against them;' and when he said this, he fell asleep." (Acts 7:60 NAB)

"Put on then, as God's chosen ones, holy and beloved, heartfelt compassion, kindness, humility, gentleness, and patience, bearing with one another and forgiving one another, if one has a grievance against another; as the Lord has forgiven you, so must you also do." (Colossians 3:12-13 NAB)

"Everything that the Father gives me will come to me, and I will not reject anyone who comes to me, because I came down from heaven not to do my own will but the will of the one who sent me. And this is the will of the one who sent me, that I should not lose anything of what he gave me, but that I should raise it (on) the last day." (John 6:37-39 NAB)

"If you forgive others their transgressions, your heavenly Father will forgive you. But if you do not forgive others, neither will your Father forgive your transgressions." (Matthew 6:14-15 NAB)

Forgiveness

While Jesus died so brutally,
even though He had sinned not,
He prayed for those who killed Him
without a second thought.
Likewise as the stones
were cast and striking Stephen,
He looked to heaven smiling,
and prayed to not get even.

Easy come, easy go;
gone with the wind,
Is forgiveness just that simple
even having gravely sinned?
Let go and let God;
bury deep the hatchet,
Love should be contagious,
let everybody catch it.
Forgive to be forgiven,
it is God's loving way,
Or else be lost in madness,
living angry every day.
If He pushes not away
one that seeks His face,
Surely, those who call for it
will end up in His grace.

"Do nothing out of selfishness or out of vainglory; rather, humbly regard others as more important than yourselves," (Philippians 2:3 NAB)

"The Lord does not delay his promise, as some regard 'delay,' but he is patient with you, not wishing that any should perish but that all should come to repentance." (2 Peter 3:9 NAB)

"I returned, and saw under the sun, that the race is not to the swift, nor the battle to the strong, neither yet bread to the wise, nor yet riches to men of understanding, nor yet favour to men of skill; but time and chance happeneth to them all. (Ecclesiastes 9:11 KJV)

"But I say to you, love your enemies, and pray for those who persecute you, that you may be children of your heavenly Father, for he makes his sun rise on the bad and the good, and causes rain to fall on the just and the unjust." (Matthew 5:44-45 NAB)

A Love Impartiality

The greatest joys are cause
for all the greatest pain.
And the more that is lost
is cause for greatest gain.
Hard working people
Struggle to get along,
And the idle and listless
Prosper doing wrong.

No glory is earned
without defeat along the way
nor are fruits of others enjoyed
when nothing has been paid.
Yet the faithful suffer always
When taken at a glance,
And all the while apparently
the sinners laugh and dance!
How is that fair
following His laws?
Justice seems illusory.
An ideal that's full of flaws.
The world makes no sense;
Anarchy appears the rule,
but understanding granted
by the Spirit wakes the fool.
His Higher Wisdom dictates
a Love impartiality.
His mercy is bountiful,
granting patience abundantly.
Given chance after chance
many ignore, refuse, and shun,
Christ reaches out a punctured hand,
Calling all and not just one.
And for this unjustified
act of ceaseless charity…?
Love knowingly like Him,
Saints must smile graciously.

† † †

"For the time that has passed is sufficient for doing what the Gentiles like to do: living in debauchery, evil desires, drunkenness, orgies, carousing, and wanton idolatry. They are surprised that you do not plunge into the same swamp of profligacy, and they vilify you;"

(1 Peter 4:3-4 NAB)

"Do not neglect the gift you have, which was conferred on you through the prophetic word with the imposition of hands of the presbyterate. Be diligent in these matters, be absorbed in them, so that your progress may be evident to everyone. Attend to yourself and to your teaching; persevere in both tasks, for by doing so you will save both yourself and those who listen to you." (1 Timothy 4:14-16 NAB)

"Just so, your light must shine before others, that they may see your good deeds and glorify your heavenly Father." (Matthew 5:16 NAB)

"Blessed be the God and Father of our Lord Jesus Christ, the Father of compassion and God of all encouragement, who encourages us in our every affliction, so that we may be able to encourage those who are in any affliction with the encouragement with which we ourselves are encouraged by God." (2 Corinthians 1:3-4 NAB)

Endowed

Stop wasting time on sinful pursuits.
Time to cultivate an abundance of fruits.

He knows it's tough, this daily grind,
Patience, child, discipline takes time.

Why do we suffer? Who says we must?
Rejoice always: His means are just.

So many tests and trials to face,
Don't despair, He gives you grace.
Though there be burdens and pain to feel,
He bolsters with love and allows us to heal.

Stride in harmony, in tune with your gifts,
His love in your heart, your spirit lifts.

Worry not about another's affair,
Yours are enough for one to bear.

You are endowed with talents galore
He has the keys, and then opens the door.

When in doubt, then don't pursue it,
But when He whispers, better do it.
With faith you enter without fear,
Time to see what will happen here.

Apply your gifts wherever you dare,
First you try, then grow, then share.

Let your light shine ever bright,
Keep the cross ever in sight.

Then every step is up and toward
The Lord, the Word, the One Adored,

Closer and closer, they don't understand,
Follow the light, and take hold of His hand.
Many will mock and might get in the way,
But carry on while bidding 'good day.'

Be a friend, but not attached,
Sometimes past doors have to be latched.

In all the times, a saint still prays
Keeping in mind the one who stays.

With Jesus active in your prayers,
Keep on climbing up those stairs.

Don't delay but don't make haste
For wonderful the surprise will taste.
Living faith with love without knowing;
His mercy, His grace forever is flowing.

† † †

"If you forgive others their transgressions, your heavenly Father will forgive you." (Matthew 6:14 NAB)

"This is the covenant that I will make with them after those days, saith the Lord, I will put my laws into their hearts, and in their minds will I write them; And their sins and iniquities will I remember no more." (Hebrews 10:16-17 KJV)

"For as the heaven is high above the earth, so great is his mercy toward them that fear him. As far as the east is from the west, so far hath he removed our transgressions from us. Like as a father pitieth his children, so the LORD pitieth them that fear him." (Psalms 103:11-13 KJV)

Divine Senility

Tears thoroughly blur your vision.
It's hard to cry out while you're under emotional distress,
sobbing uncontrollably,
bearing your pain all at once on the surface.
No one could possibly sympathize, let alone love you…
SINNER.

By some mysterious grace amid the shaking,
You find yourself crumbled to the floor,
So marvelously dispirited,
a crestfallen call penitently emerges:
Oh Lord! My God!
Forgiving, He bathes you in His Spirit
with an invisible warmth that hugs you like a child.

Although a memory remains in your time and space,
A quiet reassuring whisper echoes distinctly in your heart:

"Be not afraid, for here... I AM.
I AM now and always,"
(*older than old and wiser than wise…*)
"Remember, I forgive you… I have forgiven you… I forgave you.

So what did you say you did?
I do not remember…
But please don't forget that I forgave you."

† † †

"…And behold, I am with you always, until the end of the age." (Matthew 28:20 NAB)

"In my distress I called upon the LORD, and cried unto my God: he heard my voice out of his temple, and my cry came before him, even into his ears." (Psalm 18:6 KJV)

"Then Job began to tear his cloak and cut off his hair. He cast himself prostrate upon the ground, and said, "Naked I came forth from my mother's womb, and naked shall I go back again. The LORD gave and the LORD has taken away; blessed be the name of the LORD!" (Job 1:20-21 NAB)

"Blessed are they who mourn. They will be comforted." (Matthew 5:4 NAB)

If He Didn't Listen, He Wouldn't Respond

It has to be love that has built this bond,
and if He didn't listen, He wouldn't respond.
Once I was alone, for a friend I cried out,
And was graced from above without a doubt.
The Good Lord giveth, and He taketh it back
And though that may hurt, I know I won't lack.
Thereafter then whenever I cry,
I always get a soothing reply.
When a prayer is uttered, it then comes to mind:
A verse that speaks from God, so kind.
Too often I forget, though I don't know why,
The feeling of how He makes me fly,
'Til again I cry from far below
And He shows me again how He hears me so.
It's not just blind faith with answered prayers
That continuously remind me of how much He cares
'Cause no matter the instance, the sin, or event,
He is there with counsel when I repent.
It can only be love that has built this bond,
'cause if He didn't listen, He wouldn't respond.

† † †

"And he asked them, "But who do you say that I am?" Peter said to him in reply, "You are the Messiah."

(Mark 8:29 NAB)

"For I know well the plans I have in mind for you, says the LORD, plans for your welfare, not for woe! plans to give you a future full of hope." (Jeremiah 29:11 NAB)

"Therefore, we are not discouraged; rather, although our outer self is wasting away, our inner self is being renewed day by day. For this momentary light affliction is producing for us an eternal weight of glory beyond all comparison, as we look not to what is seen but to what is unseen; for what is seen is transitory, but what is unseen is eternal."
(2 Corinthians 4:16-18 NAB)

"His master said to him, 'Well done, my good and faithful servant. Since you were faithful in small matters, I will give you great responsibilities. Come, share your master's joy."
(Matthew 25:21 NAB)

Who Is Jesus?

Who is Jesus? To me they ask, to me?
Such a personal question; now let me see.
How can one describe the indescribable?
Or share the infinite in so short a timetable?
He's a giver of gifts, and blessings galore,
A fountain of mercy and so much more.
When my ego inflates, and I over-analyze,
Well, He's the wisdom that cuts me back down to size.
The Forgiver of sin and Redeemer by grace,
He's the reason for this smile on my face.
But to me, I wonder, is that really right?
As I consider: "to Him?" Am I even in sight?
Who is Jesus? To me they ask, to me?
As I think some more, I then clearly see,
A humble kind man, empathic toward all
Embracing a cross, getting up from each fall.
My world has been shattered, and I've felt like dying,
I've been in the pits and have just felt like crying,
I've been betrayed by friends, the closest of kind
In ways that torture and torment the mind.
I've been injured by falls and sick with disease,
And it seems as if nothing can be done with ease.
In such times of loss and sorrow and pain,
When the darkness keeps coming and coming again,
When every breath is just a sigh
And you can't help but wonder, "why???"
He's my rock that I stand on, and refuge to hide in

An ever present friend to forever confide in.
The light in my world that shines beyond measure,
And the key to unlocking all of life's treasure
He holds me together with a voice in my heart
Reassuring that nothing will cause Him to part.
He's a well-spring of hope as the source of all good things
And the melody of praise to which my heart sings:
"Through many dangers, toils, and snares I have already come,
His grace has brought me safe thus far and grace will lead me home."[6]
He's my Shepherd and root anchored way down deep,
While I'm a branch of His vine and one of His sheep.
My Jesus, My Jesus! HE KNOWS my own name,
He's called me to peace, and calls you to the same.
The God of Creation, my Jesus, our Lord!
Praise be to Him! the incarnate Word!
He is why I sleep soundly and reason for waking,
My cause to get up and joy in the making,
He's the King that I serve, and the innocent Lamb
Killed in my place so I avoid being damned.
My Jesus, My Jesus! You're all that I need,
Please give me the faith for all righteous deeds.

And Thank, YOU, forever for all that You are;
You are the ultimate model, the bright morning star.
How Amazing Your Grace and Incredible Your Spirit!
And when it's all over I'll jump when I hear it:
"My good and faithful servant, well done."
I'll shout, "Alleluia!" And into Your arms I will run!

† † †

"For whatever was written previously was written for our instruction, that by endurance and by encouragement of the scriptures we might have hope." (Romans 15:4 NAB)

"The heavens declare the glory of God; the sky proclaims its builder's craft." (Psalms 19:2 NAB)

Inspiring

The sun at rise, again at set,
Glory days when we first met,
Mountains high and oceans deep,
Friends we make and ones we keep,
Valleys low and rivers wide,
The virtues three that do abide,
Waterfalls of a sunlit hike,
Lyrics coming from the mic,
Cliffside climbs and crashing surf,
Finding out what love is worth,
Snorkeling at a coral reef,
Emotions flowing during grief,
Tears that fall in streams of joy,
Memories of a favorite toy,
The twinkle in a child's eyes,
Looking up at starlit skies,
Overcoming lifetime fears,
Wiping someone else's tears,

The smile from a pretty face,
The feeling from a warm embrace,
Friendship bonds of strongest love,
The Holy Spirit sent in a dove,
Achieving all the goals you sought,
Gratitude for what we got,
Wisdom given to be a guide,
For us all, soldiers who died,
Jesus bearing the heavy cross,
Encouraging words from the boss,
Finishing a job well done,
Watching children having fun,
Sleepless nights with deep regrets,
Wagging tails of faithful pets,
The will to stand against all odds,
Being a beloved child of God's,
Standing tall for all your rights,
The smallest dogs with largest fights,
Smiles from a kindly stranger,
Amazing tales escaping danger,
Beauty of an artless form,
Certain things outside the norm,
Heroes coming to save the day,
Watching boats across the bay,
Music that will move your soul,
Lightning's flashes and thunder's roll,
Stories that can make you think,
Strengthening your weakest link,
The rise to greatness and success,

The gentle touch of a sweet caress,
The peace that's found in simple things,
Angels with their outstretched wings,
Symbols that can ease the mind,
Random acts completely kind,
All of nature, our mother earth,
The springtime season of rebirth,
Life enduring times of sorrow,
And the hope of what may come tomorrow.

"We always give thanks to God, the Father of our Lord Jesus Christ, when we pray for you, for we have heard of your faith in Christ Jesus and the love that you have for all the holy ones" (Colossians 1:3-4 NAB)

To My Friends in Christ

As well as I am to recall,
Far back as I can see,
I know it's true I cared for you.
And for this I do agree
That as long as I am to exist,
Far forward as I can see,
I know it's true I'll care for you
And pray kindly wherever you'll be.
And now whenever I think of you,
In as much as I can see,
I know it's true I care for you,
And wish you the joy I see.

References

1. *Life Application Bible - King James Version*. Wheaton, IL: Tyndale House Publishers, 1989.
2. *The New American Bible*. *Translated from original languages with critical use of all the ancient sources and the revised New Testament authorized by the board of trustees of the Confraternity of Christian Doctrine and approved by the Administrative Committee of the National Conference of Catholic Bishops and the United States Catholic Conference.* Nashville, TN: Thomas Nelson Publishers; Catholic Bible Press, 1987.
3. Hoogasian, Michael. *Midnight Streams – Spirited Discovery of Flowing Insight 2nd ed.* A 'Sharkangel' book. Printed by Lulu.com, 2009. Available: http://stores.lulu.com/sharkangel
4. Sollier, J. (1908). The Communion of Saints. In The Catholic Encyclopedia. New York: Robert Appleton Company. Retrieved June 27, 2011 from New Advent: http://www.newadvent.org/cathen/04171a.htmCatholicCatechism
5. Catechism of the Catholic Church - Latin text copyright (c) Libreria Editrice Vaticana, Citta del Vaticano 1993.
6. Lyric from the hymn "Amazing Grace" retrieved online 2011 from "Amazing Grace: the Story of John Newton" http://www.texasfasola.org/biographies/johnnewton.html

Final Blessing:

"To all the beloved of God in Rome [and around the world], called to be holy. Grace to you and peace from God our Father, and the Lord Jesus Christ." (Romans 1:7 NAB; bracketed text added by author)

Thank you for reading my book. You can find my other writings at http://stores.lulu.com/sharkangel. I pray God's Holy Spirit has moved you to seek a deeper relationship with Him for the glory of His Holy Name.